NORFOLK DOCUMENTS 2

A HISTORY OF SWAFFHAM NATIONAL SCHOOLS

Further details of Poppyland Publishing titles can be found at
www.poppyland.co.uk
where clicking on the 'Support and Resources' button
will lead to pages specially compiled to support this book

Join us for more Norfolk and Suffolk stories and background at
www.facebook.com/poppylandpublishing

NORFOLK DOCUMENTS

Norfolk is fortunate in having a wealth of documents surviving from the past millennium. Many are cared for in the Norfolk Record Office at the Archive Centre in Norwich; others remain in private collections. Some documents (and audiovisual materials) are now available online; a few have been published in scholarly editions. However, there remain many fascinating papers known only to specialist researchers. The intent of this NORFOLK DOCUMENTS series is to bring some of these to a wider readership, taking advantage of recent short-run printing technology to present them at reasonable cost for anyone with an interest in East Anglian history.

Instead of being restricted to reproducing what the original author wrote, with all its puzzles of historical reference and sometimes of quirky handwriting, this series includes:

  careful transcriptions of the documents;
  introductions to set the originals in their historical context;
  notes to clarify obscure allusions;
  references to further reading;
  pictures, either from the original documents or from other sources;
  indexing of people, places and themes.

As with all Poppyland Publishing titles from the last few years, further resources and support materials are also being made available on the website **www.poppyland.co.uk**.

*The front of the National School as it is now, still in use as the Parish Church Rooms.
The original building, designed by W. J. Donthorn, can easily be distinguished by its
elaborate design. Compare this with the early view on page 19 and the side view on
page 20.*

NORFOLK DOCUMENTS 2

A History of Swaffham National Schools

David Butters with Olive Wilson

POPPYLAND
PUBLISHING

Copyright © 2015 estate of David Butters

First published 2015
ISBN 978-1-909796-24-9

Published by Poppyland Publishing, Cromer, NR27 9AN

Extracts from the log books are reproduced by courtesy of the headteacher of Swaffham First School. The plan of the workhouse (page 21) is from the Norfolk Record Office; all other pictures are from the author's collection.

Designed and typeset in 11 on 14 pt Goudy Old Style by
Watermark, Cromer, NR27 9ER

Printed by Lightning Source

All proceeds to Swaffham Museum

For Jasmine

Foreword

by Neil Haverson

I look upon Swaffham as my spiritual home. As a teenager I spent my formative years in the town. Each time I visit I walk around the market place dewy-eyed, stepping back in time to the late 1950s and early 1960s when I attended Hamond's Grammar School.

More recently the year 2005 stands out. I came to Swaffham to write a feature on the town for *Let's Talk* magazine. This gave me the opportunity to delve beneath the surface of places and faces I had known in my youth.

I needed to speak to someone who had in-depth knowledge of Swaffham and its history. My first port of call was the museum where I found the perfect person – someone born and bred in the town, a town councillor and local historian – David Butters. At the time he was writing a book looking at the changes in the town over his lifetime. He told me so much it became a case of what to leave out of my feature rather than what to print.

David contacted me to tell me about his next book which was to be about Swaffham's National Schools and asked if I would write the foreword. I was delighted to accept. I was so pleased when I learned the book was still to be published in spite of his sad passing.

His painstaking research takes us on a journey beginning 1553, the first record of schooling in the town. David has dipped into school log books to illustrate how education evolved. A fascinating insight to the social history of the era emerges, when parents had to pay for their children's schooling; the impact of disease and the need for children to miss school in order to help out on the farm.

We are indebted to David Butters for what he has done for the town and its history, no more so than for this permanent record of Swaffham's National Schools.

Contents

Early schools in Swaffham

After the successive invasions of the Romans, Saxons and Normans, the languages of education were that of the invaders, the elite. The poor had little or no education; this was not considered necessary, as the lower orders had no need of reading and writing. They were there to farm the land and to do as they were told.

The rulers, on the other hand, needed to learn how to read and speak Norman French and Latin, as they were the languages of the law, the court and education. It was not until the fourteenth century that, with John Wycliffe's translation, the Bible became available in English and accessible to a wider audience.

During the sixteenth century there was increasing awareness of the need for education and literacy, and the guilds in Swaffham numbered among their members at least one schoolmaster, John Sergeant, though his schoolhouse is not identified. The oldest written reference to a school in Swaffham is in a church document from the reign of Edward VI, possibly 1553, which records a payment 'for ye making and repayrying of a gram Skole hows'. (This may well refer to the old church cottage in the churchyard. Rev. G. Bouchery wrote in 1750 that this cottage, which may previously have been a guild house, was known as the schoolhouse after the suppression of the guilds in 1547; it continued to serve the town as such until 1874. It then served as a house for the verger, before in the 1980s being used for a Sunday School.)

In 1653 a little book was published in London called *A New Catechism, short and plain, . . . published for the benefit of Swaffham School, Norfolk*. Its author was George Dochant, 'master at a private school there' and takes the form of a series of questions and answers – all heavily criticizing the Roman Catholic faith.

The Churchwardens' accounts 1626–53 include items for one or two schools in 1627: 'flags for the children that are taught at the widow Sellons' and 'John

Smyths wife for the children she learneth'. A document in Swaffham Museum entitled *Remarks out of the Town Book of Repairs done to the School House* has a list of dates from 1666 to 1727. Although old, its use for research is limited as it starts 'Glazing the windows folio £4', the next entry merely 'Work & Stuff' and so every year, with the exception of 1689 when 'Tyling' is added.

In Scotland, every parish had a school from the seventeenth century, and in 1807 the House of Commons passed a bill that would have established a similar system of education in England, but the House of Lords rejected it, arguing that the interests of the Established Church were not protected. Within ten years, however, there was a National School in Swaffham, for a list of children and their classes survives in the Norfolk Record Office (DN/NDS 276). There were 61 boys and 43 girls at that time.

The Vicar, Rev. William Yonge, wrote to Rev. James Moyle in 1827 and his valuable comments on the school at that time are preserved in the Norfolk Record Office (NRO: DN 283 (7)).

> **The Rev. James Moyle**
> **Wereham**
> **Near Stoke Ferry**
> **Norfolk**
>
> Swaffham 1827
>
> Dear Sir,
>
> We have two schools here, one for boys and the other for girls, held at different places & of course under different teachers.
>
> The girls' school has been always a daily school & has been well attended, & these answers to the printed queries refer only to that. The answers to the boys' school are on the other side.
>
> Two or three years ago, from this nice attendance & other reasons, the boys' school was reduced to a Sunday school, but failing, the parents would not send their children for Sunday only. We considered, about Christmas Last, to establish a daily school again.
>
> I am afraid you must postpone your visiting the schools till another year, as both boys and girls always break up for the harvest, as their parents will not forgo their gleaning and tomorrow is the last day of keeping school, except on Sundays.

Had it been otherwise, I believe you would have found the girls school in very good order, as my own daughters and another young lady are in the habit of superintending it. But I should have no satisfaction in shewing you the boys' school, as for the reason above stated, & because the master is not so efficient as I would wish, their progress has been very slow. He is a very steady young man & has been at the National School at Norwich for instruction, but he wants energy & Support & therefore not well suited to the situation, and I do not know where to find a better.

At 74 I do not find myself so well able to attend to it as I could do formerly.

I very much approve of the form prescribed to the visitors and have no doubt it will fully answer the design of the Society.

I am your obedient servant,

Wm. Yonge

Swaffham 2nd August 1827

(Swaffham Museum has a copy of the Church of England Sunday school Institute's *Sunday school Reform Leaflet No. 1*, a leaflet for teachers, which under the heading 'Atmosphere' says that the teacher should suggest each Sunday that children should be 'orderly, attentive, quiet, industrious and reverent'. Later in the text it says the children should be 'obedient', indicative of the nature of Sunday school in the Victorian era. In the last section, marching to music with younger children is commended as 'of the greatest assistance in suggesting ideas of order and quietude'.)

The following copy of the 1828 form, answers and remarks are very similar to those for the following few years.

Questions to be answered by the Master or Mistress previous to the day of Examination, and to be delivered to the Visitors. (Form 6 is the youngest.)

6. Number who left School in the year?
42 boys, 23 girls

7. What number of children were admitted?
57 boys, 9 girls

8. Age of admission, and the age of 1st & top class?

At 7 in both schools, boys from 11 to 14. Girls from 12 to 13.

9. Do they attend school and Church regularly? Is there sufficient room in the church?

For boys see remarks on next page. Girls are in general regular both at school and Church where there are sufficient accommodations.

10. How many Children in 1st Class? Books? Progress in RK? Are they asked if they understand? Do they learn to write and cypher?

Boys 10. Testament Crossman's Catechism & prayers, learn to write & cypher. Girls 16. Testament. Questions are asked in both schools.

11. The same questions for 2nd class?

Boys 15, miracles, Crossman's Catechism. Some write & cypher.

12. do. Third Class?

Boys 19. Central School Book 2, Catechism. Some write & cipher. Girls 16 tried as the 1st class. Questions asked.

13. do. 4th Class?

Boys 19. Carols & Catechism. Some write. Girls 6. Mrs Trimmers first book for children.

14. do. 5th Class?

There are only 4 classes of boys. Girls 10 cards with four & 5 letters.

15. do. 6th Class?

Girls learn their letters.

16. Have any works of Industry been introduced into the school?

Girls are taught to sew.

17. What is the Amount of the Fund by which the School is supported and how is it raised?

The funds arise from voluntary subscriptions and an annual sermon, & of course the amount is uncertain. The Society is kind enough to give us £10.

18. Have you any remarks to make respecting the school?

See next page.

Remarks

In answer to the first part of the 9th query, I have to observe that the attendance is not so regular as might be wished.

When it is recollected that this is entirely an agricultural parish, & that the farmers expect the children to work in the fields, whenever they can find employment, the want of regularity may be accounted for, & besides, they all expect four or five weeks holidays during the Harvest gleaning.

The progress of the children under these circumstances may be considered as great as might be expected especially in the Girls School, which is regularly superintended by some ladies. In the other school the boys are oftener employed in the fields & there is not the same superintendence, as I found myself quite unable to attend to it, as I used to, & I can get no gentleman to supply my place. The master too, tho' sufficiently qualified as to knowledge has not all the energy & activity which might be wished. In what I consider as essentials I trust, the schools may be deemed efficient.

WY

Swaffham 13th February 1830

Legislation of 1833 decreed that juveniles could only be employed if they attended a school for a certain number of hours per week. As a result, from 1836 until 1871 a building in front of the former parish workhouse in the churchyard was used as a school, although from 1838 it had just been for infants up to the age of 6 years. This building was substantially altered and a spacious room added. The children were 'taught and train'd agreeably to the principles of the established Church, preparatory to their being received into the National School'. This infants' school was entirely supported by Miss Sarah Hamond of the Manor House.

A vestry minute of 12th April 1838 (preserved in the Norfolk Record Office: PD 52/76) records that a portion of the Camping Land can be used for a school 'to be conducted agreeable to the Rules & Regulations of the British & Foreign School Society' (mainly supported by non-conformist families). This did not progress further, because the rival school, that of the National Society for the Education of the Poor in the Principles of the Established Church, was almost finished. Designed by the architect W. J. Donthorn of Swaffham, it was opened on 25th June of that year on the Campingland close to Hamond's school, with 127 girls and 73 boys attending. The land purchased for the school was not very large, measuring 66 feet east to west and 51 feet 6 inches north to south. This plot cost £80, and the building nearly £500, exclusive of interior fittings. The money was raised from donations from owners of local property (resident in Swaffham or elsewhere), with the National School Society in London and Norwich giving a grant of £220 'upon condition that the business of the school be conducted upon the Madras or Bells System, combining Scriptural with Moral Education, agreeably to the Principles of the Protestant Establishment'. The cost of a master and mistress, together with running costs, were to be met from annual voluntary contributions. Mr and Mrs Wells, the master and mistress of the evening school, were appointed the school's master and mistress at a salary of £70 per annum.

A management committee included the Vicar and Curate of the parish, Miss Yonge, Mrs James and the Secretary, plus six ladies and six gentlemen elected annually from the body of the subscribers. Committee members were to attend to the general discipline of the schools and to be, in turn, weekly visitors. The vicar or curate taught scripture to the young children at least once each week.

It was probably this school which was supplied by William Sands, a builder based in Lynn Street (and the grandfather of Howard Carter). On 29th December Sands supplied:

156 feet of form @ 6½d per foot	4	4	6
7 monitors stools @ 6/6d	2	5	6
Master's writing desk	3	10	0
6 desks @ £1. 2. 6d	6	6	0
2 cupboards @ £1/ 2/ 6d	2	5	0
Coppy racks		10	6
to bracing of desks		5	6
3 dozen of brass nails		1	3
	£49	**8**	**3**

There was a charge of one penny per week but the second and other children in a family only had to pay a halfpenny. Subscribers were 'allowed to have work done gratis to the amount of the sum subscribed according to a fixed scale of prices'. The school was open every day except Saturday, which was a 'holyday'.

By December of that year it was decided to have an evening school for boys and young men employed during the day. The fees and rules were the same as for day pupils but 'no boy could be admitted to the evening school below the age of nine years'.

In the 19th century and in the early part of the 20th century, there were a number of private schools in the town advertising in trade directories, one of which was supported by a brewer, A. Morse, and other subscribers, and catered for 50 poor girls; this was a British School and is mentioned in White's Directory of 1845; it was run by the Baptists in a schoolroom built for the purpose behind the Station Street Chapel. Records exist from 1855 to 1858 (NRO: FC 100/27).

White's 1845 Directory also lists nine other 'academies' including the 'Free School', which might be Hamond's, and the National School. In 1860, Kelly's Directory describes the Baptist Chapel which had classrooms that could 'afford accommodation for 230 children'. We do not know how many actually attended. There was also a school in the Assembly Rooms, which Rev. Vince recalled as being the venue for the parish schools, 'the fee of 4d being charged'. This was based on the British School system, which was later merged into the National Schools and the fees lowered.

A hand-written notebook in Swaffham museum (no. 1128), of uncertain age and different authors but believed to date mainly from the late 19th century, is a valuable reference book for various subjects, including schools. One author had this to say:

Mr. Wells and his wife must have come early in the [18]30's. Mrs Webb went to school in Mantry Yard paying 6d a week. Afterwards she went to Mrs. Wells at the Assembly Rooms.

Evening school for girls sewing was held in a room built out from the Clerk's house in the churchyard. Miss Agnes Yonge taught sewing in the Wednesday afternoon school in the Assembly Rooms. Miss Dalton taught there, assisted by Jane Walpole.

Throughout Lent, children went to church on Fridays to say the Catechism.

The Schoolmaster before Mr Wells was James Philo, who was also Clerk and shoemaker. He also taught in the Assembly Rooms and a Sunday school was there too. He lived in Church House, and the 'Girls evening school and Sunday school was held in a room adjoining now pulled down'.

The little private schools came and went, leaving scarce a trace behind them of their existence. In *Price Above Rubies* (1965), Ursula Bloom describes the education of her mother Polly Gardner (born 1860) in Swaffham during the mid-Victorian era:

> Through their early years the girls attended day school. There was Mrs. Tranter, an amiable old dear, widowed and with a couple of daughters to support, which was her only qualification for teaching! At first Fanny [Ursula's grandmother] liked her, then paid an unexpected visit. Mrs. Tranter, sitting in her high chair facing the class, had been nodding, and was taken by surprise. Mrs. Tranter stumbled when she curtseyed to Mamma. Fanny had shrewd eyes, and recognised the fact that nobody worried too much here about lessons. Shocking, said she, I'm paying for nothing.
>
> 'Bonnets and cloaks dears, we're going home,' she announced.
>
> Next it was Mrs. Trundle's (for daughters of gentlemen, only). She had gin in her desk, for she tippled outrageously, and one afternoon Fanny found this out. She marched in on another surprise visit, to find Mrs. Trundle with cap awry and cameo brooch undone. 'Wotch you doing here?' she asked Fanny.
>
> 'You're drunk,' said Fanny, and home she went with the little girls.
>
> There were three more schools, then they went to Miss Hunt's. Here they learnt something, for Miss Hunt was a blue-stocking. 'So sad,' said Fanny, 'for like that she can never hope to marry.' Eventually trouble began. Miss Hunt did not appreciate Fanny's impromptu visits, or being asked questions before the class. So she asked Fanny questions. The class was English Literature, about which Fanny knew nothing, but she was not going to say so. Oh no, not Fanny! When Miss Hunt asked her how she felt about Chaucer she replied that she thought him rather old-fashioned! Miss Hunt arched her eyebrows, and Fanny lost her temper. Once more bonnets and cloaks were called for.

The above may be part fact, part fiction, but there is a lot of truth in it about the way the Dame schools were run and a Miss Hunt is recorded in a Kelly's Directory of the time.

Another author was Dr Catherine B. Firth, who had a long and distinguished career as a teacher and lecturer. She wrote in her autobiography (*Night Bells,*

1966) of her education in Swaffham in the large house known as Cranglegate. Here she spent most of her childhood (after being orphaned) being taught with her sister by an aunt who happened to have been a teacher. The aunt must have been a good teacher and the child a good student, because Catherine went on to lecture in History at both Cambridge and Oxford.

An early twentieth-century century Dame school is recalled by Christine Chalcraft, née Thompson, who recalls going to Shirley House, then occupied by the Harbord family. The class was small, and the teacher favoured the girls of the Hamond family, who lived in the Manor House and were related to the Harbords. Christine recalled that when any of the children wanted to use the toilet, they went into a room with a chamber pot in it and were supervised by a grim-faced old lady, dressed in black bombazine and lace. This was obviously a great deterrent, because as soon as there was a break in lessons, the children rushed outside and used the bushes in the garden. Christine learnt more about boys this way than was ever explained in the classroom.

The Infants' School

According to the notebook in Swaffham museum, the Infants' School was opened in September 1838

> in part of the house formerly the Rectory, and for near a century past, the Parish Workhouse, which had been at this present time altered and renewed at very considerable expense & a spacious room most conveniently & substantially fitted for the occasion.

> The children are to be taught & train'd agreeably to the principles of the established church, & preparatory to their being received into the National School.

> The expense of altering & rebuilding the room & for conducting the Business of the school is done at the sole charge of Miss Sarah Hamond of Swaffham & eldest daughter of the late Anthony Hamond Esq. of Westacre High House in this County.

The National Schools

Swaffham National School opened on 25th June 1838. 'Nod's College', as it was known to many of the boys who passed through its doors and lived to tell the tale, still stands today, but serves another purpose as the Parish Church Rooms.

The date stone of the building

The old boys who remember it today knew a quite different school from the one which first opened over 160 years ago, for 350 pupils. One of the many differences was that until 1901 this building also housed the girls' school on the upper floor. The age range of the children there was different too. They

A view of the building on the Campingland, as it appeared around the end of the nineteenth century.

Side view of the National School prior to construction of Goodrick Place.

were supposed to leave the Infants' School and start at the National School at the age of 6 years – although in 1850 complaints were made because children were being kept in the Infants' School 'until 8 and 9 years of age'. They then entered the National School 'at an age at which they are very soon taken away to work'.

The first headmaster, Mr Wells, was a retired turnkey (warden) from the local jail. He was succeeded by Richard Haycox ,who started the boys' log book on 11th March 1863. On 8th February 1864 Mr Cotterill was a substitute head until 22nd February 1864, when William Pheasant was appointed. Mrs Pheasant taught the girls. Under the monitorial system pioneered by Joseph Lancaster and Andrew Bell, pupil teachers and monitors helped assistant masters so that fewer teachers were needed. All the boys were taught in one room and the girls in another, so building costs were kept down.

The Church had a very firm grip on the education of the poor and this is reflected in the rules of the school in the early days. The aim of the early National Schools was to ensure people knew their place in the social order, especially as most of the pupils came from the labouring classes. School in those early days of Victoria's reign was more an instrument of social control than of proper education. The National Schools and the British and Foreign Schools Society were Church-controlled, with the local vicar or the curate visiting almost every day to give lessons and even to examine the children. There was an annual visit from the Diocesan Inspector, whose principal task

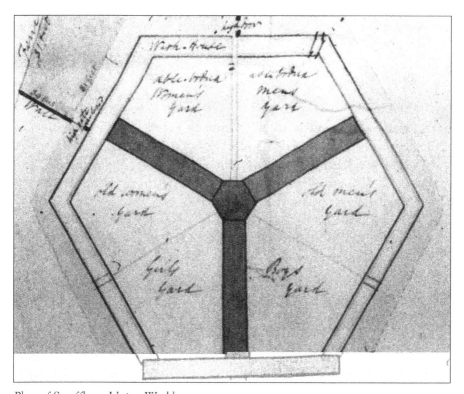

Plan of Swaffham Union Workhouse.
Note how families are split up by confining different sexes to different yards.

was to ensure religious education was being taught in accordance with the requirements.

This attitude was also evident in the Union workhouse schoolroom, where the education was basically to give the children moral training, not to encourage them to improve their lot, just to accept the station in life they had been born into. This was drilled into them from the early years in the workhouse, then later in the National Schools. The teachers were largely untrained and poorly paid.

As in other fields of Victorian Society, there were reformers, people with a social conscience and in Norfolk one such reformer provided the first lesson books for the workhouse school in 1836 and recommended that the schoolmaster, John Pratt, was trained to a better standard. This was not a popular idea, because education of the poor depended upon the benevolence of the gentry, clergy, and those with the money to help, but it was precisely those people who benefited most from a subservient and ill-educated working class.

Nevertheless, it is likely that workhouse schooling in Swaffham was as good as the rest of the county – the Poor Law Commissioners in 1843 reported that Norfolk provided 'an unusually good system of pauper education'.

By 1897, the Local Government Board had decided to issue a list of Orders relating to the education of poor children and these included:

> **ARTICLE II. . . . every child in good health between the ages of three and seven years should receive, during the ordinary school hours, at least three hours of instruction every day and every child in good health between the ages of seven and fourteen years, during the ordinary school hours, at least four hours of instruction every day.**

(Note the use of the word 'instruction' rather than 'education'.)

Girls had needlework lessons:

> **at least two-thirds shall be occupied in plain needlework, knitting, and cutting out and making garments, and not more than one-third in mending. . . .**
>
> **ARTICLE IX. . . . instruction, religious instruction, industrial training, manual or industrial work. . . .**
>
> **ARTICLE XI. . . . 'Instruction', except in the term 'Religious Instruction', means instruction in any of the subjects for which grants may be made under the Code of Regulations of the Education Department for the time being in force except cookery, laundry work, dairy work, or cottage gardening.**

Workhouse children however, were not welcome in the National Schools. The managers of the school stated in a letter to the workhouse guardians that they would rather not receive these children, but would not refuse to do so. The Education Department, however, decided that if there were room, the workhouse children must be admitted. These children had to pay more than the other pupils – a curious state of affairs when we consider that the reason many of them were in the workhouse was because their family was in debt. It seems as if the school managers decided on this higher charge to deter poor children from attending school. However, these children may have had some of their fees paid from grants received by the Guardians of the workhouse. It may also be that the school charged more because the child might have been from another parish.

A private school

The lessons described above are in stark contrast to those taught at the private 'Classical and Mathematical School' (headmaster Leonard Russell Goggs, who lived in the Mansion House, later to be replaced by the Corn Exchange). In a school report in Swaffham Museum's possession, the number in the class was 13 and the lessons were – English Subjects, Arithmetic (including mental arithmetic), algebra, Euclid, Latin, French, Greek, Shorthand, Bookkeeping, Elocution and Writing. There is no room for manual or industrial work – these boys were simply not expected to dirty their hands. Neither was there a way for a bright workhouse boy or girl to gain a scholarship and improve their education.

It is little wonder then that Nicholas Hamond's wish in his will that £500 be used to build a school to teach 'twenty poor boys reading and writing' and another £500 to build a 'house of Industry' (workhouse) next to it, was not adhered to. True, a school was built; this took in fee-paying boarders as well as the original 20 free places. In contrast, a rule of Swaffham included a paragraph referring to the fact that 'No children are, or indeed can be, employed in the fields owing to the necessity for school attendance. Though the boys begin to work directly they leave school, and are paid about 4/- a week at first.'

The Classical and Mathematical School with headmaster Leonard Goggs.

A Church Central School proposal

A leaflet in Swaffham Museum refers to the 1936 Education Act and the fact that Swaffham had been chosen for the building of a Church Central School. The area covered by this school would encompass ten elementary Church schools, including Swaffham. The leaflet is also an appeal for financial support, for 25% of the cost, as £2,000 had to be raised 'before 31st July 1938'. Although over £1,200 had been given or promised, the appeal must have failed to meet its target, as this school, with the aim that it 'should continue the religious teaching in which they have been grounded in their Junior Schools', was not built.

The log books

Although log books had been in use for a number of years, it was the 'New Code' in 1895 that defined more precisely what should be entered and who was responsible for the provision of and the care of such books: the book should be kept by the principal teacher, 'who is required to enter into it from time to time such events as the introduction of new books, apparatus, or courses of instruction, any plan of lessons approved by the Inspector, the visits of managers, absence, illness, or failure of duty on the part of any of the school staff, or any special circumstances affecting the school, that may for the sake of future reference or for any other reason, deserve to be recorded. No reflections or opinions of a general character are to be entered in the log book.'

In the Swaffham National School log books it is recorded that the pupil teachers were a mixed blessing. Two pupil teachers were reprimanded several times for hitting boys' ears in class. Another was spoken to about knocking a boy about the head with a book. It was a hard time for some pupil teachers, though; W. P. Coe was persistently late for his own lessons in the morning and on 7th October 1896 the log book notes:

> **W. P. Coe 4 minutes late for his lessons this morning. I have been obliged to discontinue setting him any work to get up on Tuesday & Thursday nights. He goes to the technical school on those days by the 5 p.m. train, returning at 9 p.m., after which he cannot do lessons for me, as he is not in a fit state. The lad's work is done as if he were in a dazed condition & he seems to have no energy for teaching while his lessons for me are very badly done.**

A few days later he was again late for lessons and when he arrived the door had been bolted. The master bolted it at 8 minutes past 7 a.m. Even so, the next year Coe obtained a first class pass in the Queen's Scholarship Examination.

Amongst the children, mumps and measles regularly swept through the school; in 1894 all schools were closed for 4½ weeks due to measles, which meant that 300 children were away. Even though they could be fatal, they were relatively minor complaints compared with the dreaded scourges of scarlet fever and consumption (tuberculosis) that killed off so many of the children.

Scarlet fever was responsible for many deaths. In 1882 medical authorities closed the school for a while because of the prevalence of this disease and there was another epidemic in 1893 that threatened to close the school again. Other killer diseases noted in the school log books were diphtheria and typhoid.

Influenza was another common illness. In 1892 there were 300 cases of it in the town, whose population then was only about 3,000, so one in ten had the flu.

The causes of these epidemics were many. In 1868 it was reported that there was 'a great deal of sickness in the town. The doctors ascribe this to drinking the water from the taps.'

Conditions at home were hard. In the winter it was not uncommon for children to be away from school because they could not get their boots on because of chilblains. One young lad was away one morning because his boots were being mended and he had no others.

Accidents, too, took their toll of young lives. John Crickling died from lock-jaw (tetanus). After leaving school on 22nd September 1884, he was riding with the driver on the goods delivery truck of the Great Eastern Railway when, near his home, 'he got down while the horse was trotting & becoming entangled in the wheel, was much injured about the knee, foot & great toe. After lingering nearly three weeks, lock-jaw set in.'

There were severe difficulties in getting to school in the winter. In fact the roads were in a pretty poor state in winter even without any snow or ice to add to the problems. 'Roads in a terrible state' is a not uncommon remark found during the winter months.

A particularly dreadful day came on 19th January 1880:

> **The gale of yesterday has made immense drifts in the roads, increased by the snowfall during the night. The roads are impassable, & it is impossible in many cases for children to get to school.**

> **On the railway men were employed the whole night till daybreak clearing the snowdrifts in the cuttings. The first train this morning from Swaffham to Lynn was snowed up in the Narborough cutting & was not extricated for several hours.**

In some cases where tradesmen's carts went out yesterday, they could not get back till today. The mail cart could not go to Brandon last night, nor did any come from Litcham or Rougham. No letters have been received from London or the provinces this morning. Attendance at school in the morning and afternoon was small.

Bad weather was also experienced in June 1889, when a terrific storm raged in the town and neighbourhood.

Hail & rain accompanied the thunder & lightning. Some hailstones measured four & half inches in circumference. An immense number of windows were broken in the town & the windows on the south side of the school were wrecked.

A few years later, a hurricane struck one Sunday afternoon, which stripped many houses of their tiles. The school lost some slates, but did not sustain much damage.

Work was another reason for much absenteeism. Osier peeling, crow scaring, walnut gathering, hay making and harvest time all meant that boys were away from school at one time of the year or another. The time of harvest depended upon the weather, so the school holidays were variable. In 1894 the head keeper at Cockley Cley brought a note from Mr Cooper at the Hall asking for children to go 'brushing' (beating) on the estate. There was quite a fuss about it and the Master sent a note to the attendance officer with the names of 10 boys who had gone.

In 1878, on 8th April, Mr Pheasant wrote:

In consequence of the strike of farm labourers in the parish, a large number of children have been sent by their parents into the agricultural gangs.

Farms and distributive trades were the mainstays of the local, quite self -contained, economy then. This can be seen by a list of occupations taken up by boys leaving in 1894:

printer's boy 2; errand boy 7; clerk 3; office boy 3; farm work 11; cabinet maker 1; foundry boy 1; baker's boy 2; doctor's boy 1; shoemaker 1; left town 2. Total 34.

At first, the new 1880 Education Act, which made it compulsory for children to attend school until the age of ten, did little to alter absenteeism. Later that year, our headmaster tells us the act 'remains a dead letter in the town. A census of children was taken but nothing further has been done. Children on whom warnings had been served take no notice, & go to work or play about as they had previously done.' Things changed as the Education Act was applied, and on one occasion 27 Swaffham parents were summoned before the magistrate for sending their children to school irregularly, or neglecting to send them at all.

The vicar or his curate taught religious knowledge and every child was expected to attend Sunday school. Those who did not could be expelled from school, as could those who did not attend the Church of England Sunday school. The names of three such boys, William Clark, John Clark and Isaiah Webb, appear on 21st June 1869 with the words 'left on account of the Sunday rule'. The next year Alfred and Albert Bone left rather than attend the Sunday school.

The boys attended church on other occasions too; for example, in 1869 they attended church on the Monday before Easter and they attended each morning throughout Passion Week. There was a holiday on Good Friday, but they were at church again on Easter Monday, having the afternoon off and they did the same on Easter Tuesday. On Saints' days the boys were in church again, celebrating such saints as St Luke the Evangelist on 18th October and the Festival of St Simon and St Jude.

During Michaelmas Week, almost every year, boys left and new ones arrived. This was due to the annual change round of farm workers, who had a one-year contract from one Michaelmas to another and at the end of that time often had to look elsewhere for employment.

An unusually large number of boys left in 1872 when several families from the town and neighbourhood emigrated in search of a better life in America. A general agricultural depression and the opening up of new frontiers with innumerable opportunities in the brave new world over the ocean encouraged many families to leave.

On 11th May 1872 'all the children presented today passed in reading, writing and arithmetic', so the three R's were well taught by then.

Exams were taken in March with one examiner being the Diocesan Inspector and others being School Managers who conducted the drawing exam in conjunction with the Science and Art Department. Prizes were awarded to those who did well. It was unusual for the school to get a bad report from the

Diocesan Inspector, even in years when the government inspector criticised the school.

It was not until 1876 that the children were examined in such subjects as Geography, Grammar and English History. These changes were brought about under the Education Act of 1876. About that time there was a marked reduction in the recorded occasions when the boys attended church and visits to the school by the clergy, indicating an increasing influence of the state upon education.

Even though there were bright boys in the school, it was not until 1896 that a scholarship for the fee-paying Hamond's School, given by Mr H. Lee Warner, was awarded to the boys in the National School. This first scholarship was won by Luther Layern, who, two years later, was the only boy in East Anglia to gain 1st class honours in the Cambridge Preliminary local Examination.

The ability of the boys seemed to be in spite of, rather than because of, the early schooling they received. This was not the fault of the Infants' school though, as many cases are recorded of children not starting school until they were 6 or 7 years of age. Another reason was the Dame schools referred to earlier, run by untrained, often single, women with no proper experience of teaching. Frequently, they were little more than child minders until the child was old enough to attend the National School on the Campingland. There are many reports of intakes from the Infants' school being backward in many respects. In 1894, 14 out of 54 were sent back because they only just knew their letters.

It seems as if some former pupils bore a grudge against the school, for on 5th November 1887 '56 quarries of glass were broken in the boys' classroom window. A gun being discharged at the window caused the damage.'

The culprits were caught and two days later appeared at the Petty Sessions in the Shirehall, William Winter, a higgler of Lynn Street and Thomas Spencer, blacksmith, also of Lynn Street, were both charged with damaging the windows. The injury was caused with an old rifle without parts of the firing mechanism. Winter held the rifle and Spencer struck the cap with a hammer. Winter was fined £2 including costs and damage, and Spencer £1 10s including costs & damage.

Life was not all hardships and toil; school life had its lighter side and there were holidays, which lasted for a month at harvest time and a fortnight at Christmas. There were also odd days and half days at Easter and Whitsun and on special occasions such as the marriage of the vicar's daughter, when the children gathered at the school at 3.30 for free buns.

The fair in town also warranted a holiday, probably because the boys would have been away anyway.

Obviously, it did not need much to cause the boys to be away. On 13th January 1865 the master having to write 'Attendance in the morning small, owing to the Prince of Wales passing through the town'; this was a major event for Swaffham. The Prince was back again on 5th December 1888, arriving in Swaffham by the 3.42 p.m. train on his way to visit Mr Amherst MP at Didlington Hall. About 30 horsemen escorted the Prince through the town and the houses of many people were decorated. Several boys were away in the afternoon to see the procession. (The Prince would have passed the new Corn Exchange, with its attractive architectural style. This may have inspired the Prince to commission the same builders, Goggs Bros of Swaffham, to build the new Sandringham House.)

Another big event was the Norfolk Agricultural Show, not permanently stationed just outside Norwich as it is now, but a nomadic show, moving along the Lynn–Norwich road, stopping one year at Dereham, another at Lynn and, as in 1876 and 1889, Swaffham. The boys had two days holiday for each of those. How many actually went to the show is another matter. School was kept until 11.30 a.m. on both days.

The annual church Sunday school treat was another occasion when there were free buns – together with a good tea, presents of clothing and an orange. This led to considerable absenteeism on the afternoon on which they were held. The Baptists, the Wesleyans and the Primitive Methodists all had treats at various times, sometimes all together.

In 1882 the children of the Sunday school had their treat with the juvenile members of the Church of England Temperance Society in the Vicarage Field. They were entertained by a steam roundabout, had tea and 'played 'til dusk'.

The school treat itself was an eagerly awaited part of the school year. At first there is no record of the children actually going anywhere, just an annual summer treat, attended in 1876 by some 400 children. Eventually the children did have outings and Castle Acre was a very popular place to go, the children playing amongst the ruins and thoroughly enjoying themselves. They were taken there in wagons and wagonettes lent by local farmers and must have been a marvellous sight trundling down the road waving their flags. Modern technology had caught up with the school treat by 1897, because then the girls were taken in three wagons pulled by one of Mr Stratton's traction engines and the boys were in another three wagons pulled by one more traction engine. Two other wagons pulled by two horses completed the procession.

Demonstrations, too, meant that the children were absent. In 1874 when the labourers marched in procession through the town carrying flags and accompanied by a brass band many children were away and attended a tea held by the demonstrators.

The Queen's Golden and Diamond Jubilees were celebrated with holidays, as was Prince Albert Victor's coming of age.

Probably the most momentous occasion for the local children occurred when it was written:

> The children came to the school this afternoon, & at 3 p.m. marched to the railway station, accompanied by the Revs. A. R. Gwyn & B. G. Smith, to meet Capt. Wilson, of Her Majesty's ship Hecla, who returned from the war in the Sudan. A public reception took place, & the town was gaily decorated with flags etc. A procession consisting of the rifle corps, the pensioners, carriages of the gentry & the school children escorted Capt. Wilson to his mother's house. The children carried their flags. The registers were not marked.

Capt. Arthur Knyvett-Wilson had just been awarded the Victoria Cross.

In the severe winter of 1947, due to the low temperatures, the pipes inside froze up and in the morning the boiler blew up. The boys were then sent to the Corn Exchange for lessons.

The National School closed in 1955 and the girls' school buildings became part of Swaffham Junior and Infants School when Swaffham Secondary Modern School opened.

Boys' School 1863–1955

Summary of log book entries 1863–1916

At the start of the log book on 11th March 1863 the Master was Richard H. Haycox. On 8th February Mr Cotterill substituted for Mr Haycox, who was never seen again. On 17th February, the Committee met to consider the appointment of a schoolmaster. Mr Pheasant was chosen, and commenced duties on 22nd February 1864. Old Testament lessons were part of the curriculum, usually taken by the Curate, this being a National School, run under rules made by the

Church of England. As with the girls' school, the boys attended church on all the saints' days, and especially at Easter.

1864

Notices were sent to the parents on 15th February stating that the children must be at school by 9 o'clock. This was in many cases a futile exercise, as many parents could neither read nor write. Punishments were meted out for lying several times. Attendance was small because of bad weather in the winter.

The boys from the Union workhouse were withdrawn from school on 17th June 1864, as there was now a master in the workhouse.

One boy was punished for taking bribes off boys instead of sending them from their class (possibly for punishment).

The attendance was small on 27th September, owing to the Rifle Band being on the Market.

On 24th October, the Lord Bishop of Norwich attended the school and examined the upper classes in their knowledge of the Bible, Catechism and Liturgy.

1865

Attendance was small on 13th January because the Prince of Wales was passing through the town. (The same comment was made in the girls' register.) A low attendance due to heavy snow and rain meant that only 65 boys were there when the Diocesan Inspector called. From 20th June, the number of boys attending both in the morning and afternoon were recorded in the log book.

An Inspector commented that 'the boys' and girls' schools are doing very well'.

On 11th September 1865 a new rule was introduced, stating that children who attended the day school must also attend the Sunday school. The boys attended church to pray for the Lord's help during the cattle plague, as did the girls.

1866

Her Majesty's Inspector noted on 20th July 1866 that the work of the school was satisfactory on the whole, but the reading throughout ought to be better. Attendance on 14th August was small, so it was thought advisable to begin the Harvest Vacation.

1867

On the afternoon of Sunday 23rd June, William Murrell was drowned in Mr Dutchman's Pit on the Westacre Road.

On 4th October, Rev. J. Fraser held a meeting at the school to consider what steps should be taken to better the conditions of the agricultural labourers and their children.

Several children were away on the 22nd October, gathering and cleaning walnuts.

Three children were taken off the registers, two because of the Sunday Rule and one other because his father would not allow him to learn the catechism.

In December, children who had been working in the agricultural gangs attended school because the snow was heavy and they could not work outside.

1868

Several boys were crow scaring on 9th March, and because of the mild weather others were in the agricultural gangs.

An evening school was also run, although records are not available. Rev. Salisbury Everard, Rev. V. Houchen, Rev. A. H. Paine and Mr. Plowright examined this school of 50 boys on 26th March. After the examination, the boys were given a supper at school.

On 2nd April the log book records a great deal of sickness, ascribed to water from the taps.

From 15th April until 27th May, work came before school with the boys who did osier peeling. When it was wet, they were allowed to come to school.

On 16th June the gang boys were once again at school because the ground was too hard and dry to work, due to lack of rain for a very long time.

Scarletina was a fatal disease for some; on 7th November Fredrick Butters died of the disease. His brother Stephen also had the disease, but survived. Others died at this time too. In 1870, one of the pupil teachers was away for eleven weeks with scarletina. This had affected the school for a year.

1869

A new school bell was fixed on 9th July.

In one of the first reports recorded from an inspector, it was said that 'the schools are in a state of great efficiency'.

During Michaelmas, several boys were away helping their family move house when the father had to move to another farm. (It was the custom for labourers to be employed on an annual contract.) One boy left school to become a page to a lady in Leeds.

1870

At springtime, several boys went into the gangs. At this time, measles and scarletina were both prevalent in the town. The measles was very prevalent for a long time, but the numbers increased again on 30th May.

About 260 girls and boys, including the Sunday scholars, attended the school annual treat on 28th July.

An unusual entry on 15th September tells us that the children had the afternoon off because of the 'Cottagers' Show'. This may have been the forerunner of the horticultural show, as the next year it is described as the 'Cottagers' Flower Show'.

Rev. Salisbury Everard commented on the need for new books.

The New Education Act was considered at a meeting of the ratepayers on 7th November, so the boys had a half-day holiday in order that the master could attend the meeting.

1871

A persistent truant was Rev. E. G. Darby, who should have attended school to take scripture lessons. On one occasion, the junior Curate was out shooting rather than attending school. Mr Pheasant noted his non-attendance each time. One entry, on 31st January, recorded that Mr Darby had not been at the school since the holiday (9th January); he had not attended regularly since October. In the end, Mr Darby left Swaffham on 16th February. His successor, Rev. Mr Dennison, was more conscientious.

Despite the new Education Act, when the weather was mild on 6th March, Mr Pheasant noted that 'several boys had gone into the gangs'.

On 8th March, Rev. S. Everard and Mr Plowright examined the boys in science and art.

266 boys and girls had their annual treat on 10th August.

A Diocesan inspector reported that the boys 'do their work very fairly, considering the irregularity of attendance'. Also 'the offices of the boys' school require attention'.

The night school commenced on 23rd October 1871, probably because this school was for boys who worked in the day on the gangs and in October the nights were too dark for them to work. Mr W. Walker managed this as the committee considered that 'both schools were too much for the master's health'.

Visits from Mr Dennison became fewer and fewer, until he left Swaffham about 29th November to go with the vicar, Rev. Salisbury Everard to Burgate, Suffolk. The new vicar was Rev. H. Wright, and the new curate Rev. T. J. Hardman visited the school on 4th December (for the first time on a weekday). The curate and the vicar regularly visited to give lessons on Bible subjects.

1872

The Vicar died suddenly on 11th March. He was succeeded by Rev. G. R. Winter on 8th April.

Osier peeling meant that several boys were absent from the 23rd April.

280 boys and girls attended the annual treat on 7th August, during which it rained nearly all the time, with thunder and lightning.

1873

The 'new classrooms' were commenced on 24th March.

On 8th April there was a strike by farm labourers which meant that a large number of children were sent to work in the agricultural gangs by their parents.

Several families from the town and neighbourhood emigrated to America; six boys and girls who would have been eligible for examination by the school inspector left the town between 1st and 27th May.

At the same time, several boys were away osier peeling.

The Science and Art department gave 11 prizes as a result of an examination.

Governors inspected the school and reported on the Master, saying 'Mr Pheasant takes great pains with the school and the boys do their work well'.

August 1st was a memorable day, as new desks were brought to the school, and the new classrooms were finished on 7th August.

The new Infants school opened for the first time on 15th September and on 23rd 16 boys under the age of 7 years were sent to it, while six boys were sent from the Infants School to the Boys' School.

A new brand, with the letters SNS, was received to mark slates with.

An entry on 10th November records that the opening between the school and the house to the north belonged to the school and was previously part of the schoolyard.

1874

John Walker, formerly a boy of this school, and then in the employ of Mr T. G. Smith, grocer, died after a short illness on 24th March. He lived with his grandfather, Mr Dixon, a turnkey at the Bridewell.

Sixteen children entered the school on 27th April from the Infants' school.

There is a reference to 'F. & Jas. & Benj. Ship' and Herbert Green emigrating to America with relatives.

The price of tuition of all children at the school rose from 1d per week, to 2d per week for both boys and girls. Originally, brothers or sisters were allowed to attend for half that of their older brother or sister.

On 16th July about 400 boys, girls and infants attended the school treat after a short service at church.

The labourers, accompanied by a brass band, marched through the town carrying flags on the 23rd July. Many schoolchildren were there and a free tea was held later.

Building work commenced at the school on 27th July, making the classrooms 15 feet longer and the main rooms 8 feet longer, but when the school reassembled in September after the summer holiday, the work was not complete and boys and girls had to work together in the same room. The girls went back to their own rooms on 27th September. During this time, the old gas fittings were removed and new ones fixed. A new staircase to the girls' rooms, coalhouse, cap room for the boys and closets were added during the building work. The gasfitters were there though, with carpenters and workmen making so much noise that boys could not be heard reading to the master.

On 20th November, with the consent of the Trustees of the Town Estate, swings, parallel bars, horizontal bar and a seesaw were erected on the Campingland for the use of the boys of the school.

1875

On 16th March the governors met to discuss raising the fees to keep the school going; unless an appeal was made to the parishioners, it was claimed, the schools could not go on, but the proposal to raise the pence was rejected.

History, Geography and Grammar were introduced to the curriculum from

3rd May according to a new code brought in this year. The timetable had to be deviated from in some respects.

On 13th July labourers held a demonstration in the town, with flags and a band. The attendance was smaller than usual.

On 23rd July the 'Clown Cricketers' played a match at the school (on the Campingland?) and there was a half-day holiday in the afternoon.

The tickets of the Clothing Club were distributed on 5th October by Miss Day.

Michaelmas, when boys moved to other villages and towns, also saw the departure of one boy who had gone into the workhouse because the Board had stopped his mother's outdoor relief.

On 19th November new burners were fitted to the gaslights, as the old ones had given insufficient light.

1876

On 13th April 1876 there was snow to the depth of seven or eight inches (18–20 cm), continuing to fall all day. The master was helping the children of the infants' school. The Crown Omnibus was used to help to convey the children. In the afternoon a half day's holiday was given. The weather had been cold all week.

Mr Pheasant was commended in the school inspector's report (entered in the log book on 12th June). He was said to 'well and conscientiously teach the boys and the result does him much credit'. However, the young children who had entered straight from the streets did not do as well as those who had passed through the Infants' School.

The Norfolk Agricultural Show was held at Swaffham on 14th and 15th June.

About 400 boys, girls and Infants attended the annual treat on 9th August, with fine and hot weather.

1877

On 17th January Sgt Instructor Johnson of G Company, 3rd Norfolk Rifle Volunteers, took the boys in drill, as recommended by HM Inspector.

Two new harmoniums were purchased on 28th February, one for the girls and one for the boys, as a result of part of a small legacy to the school by Miss Dolynon. A new organ in the church was opened on 5th April.

An entry on 13th June notes that a former pupil teacher, whose results in examinations were always good, died in London of consumption on the 8th June. He was only 21 years old. He was buried in the churchyard.

On 19th July in the parish church the Lord Bishop of Norwich confirmed several pupil teachers from the schools.

Labourers demonstrated in the town on 24th July. They paraded the town with flags and a brass band.

Drill Sergeant Johnson took the boys in drill on 7th August; he had to go to Norwich the next day to be at the Battalion shooting.

For the first time, the girls and boys rooms were painted and coloured during the holiday, at a cost of £23 3s 0d.

At the school treat on 25th September, the children did not attend Divine Service in the church because workmen were erecting a new reredos (screen) in the church.

William Coe, a former pupil teacher, was appointed assistant master at a large school in Tunstall, Staffordshire.

1878

The 1876 Education Act was being brought into effect, but an entry on 18th March records that the books used did not yet have the relevant forms for obtaining particulars such as date of birth etc.

The school inspectors called on 8th April and commenced examination of all the children, but many of the elder boys had worked until 2 o'clock.

The osier-peeling season had begun on 16th May, when the School Attendance Officer visited. Several children who should not have been there were employed. The employer, Mr Jarvis, was visited and those children were discharged.

The Inspector's report stated that the boys' school is 'evidently taught with great care'.

It was noted on 19th July that the Education Act remained a dead letter in the town; children disregarded warnings.

On 22nd July the Labourers demonstrated again in the town, with flags flying.

A pupil teacher, William Crookham, who started at the school in May, was absent in the morning of 23rd July, because 'he did not wake himself in time'. On 9th October his reason was he 'overslept himself'. He had a day off on 13th December because of illness, but was seen skating on the Pool later. He was repeatedly warned about talking in school.

1879

William Coe was spoken to again on 18th April about talking to another pupil teacher. 'Very sleepy' was his excuse for not coming into school late at 9 a.m. on 30th September.

On 16th September, F. Avis (pupil teacher) was absent from Scripture lessons commencing at 7.30 a.m. The reason given was that he went fishing early and did not get home in time.

A third entry (on 29th November) criticised the Education Act as being a dead letter despite the clerk and school attendance officer receiving £65 for assembling statistics, but with nothing whatever being done.

On 9th December mumps were going through the school. Because of the severe weather, several children were also away with chilblains, being unable to get their boots on.

The Downham and Swaffham Rifle Corps had a shooting match on 25th June 1879. The Drill sergeant had to change the days he took drill in order to accommodate this.

Measles swept through the school from the 16th July and many children were affected. This continued until 22nd August, when the school broke up for Harvest Holiday a week early because of the measles epidemic.

During the harvest holiday, a great alteration was made in the drainage of the school, when a pipe ran under the school and emptied into a ditch on the other side of the Campingland. (The ditch ran eventually into a pond near the crossroads of Sporle Road and New Sporle Road.)

On 6th October, W. Crookham was at school until 4.15 apparently as well as usual, but an hour afterwards sent a certificate signed by Mr Marriot (surgeon) stating that Crookham had injured his back and was not fit to continue his occupation. On 7th October he went home to Docking and a week later a letter was received from his father saying that he must lie on his back for three months by order of the doctor because of injuries to his spine. He returned on 5th January 1880.

Several children away on 8th October because of the teas given by the different drapers of the town. This was on the same day as the clothing coupons were given out.

In consequence of the Harvest Thanksgiving in the church, a tea and meeting afterwards were arranged by the Church of England Temperance Society.

1880

An entry on 6th January refers to the parents of four boys and four girls being summoned to appear before the magistrate for irregular attendance. Orders were made for the attendance of all, with the exception of one child, who was ill. Colds & sore throats and the after-effects of the measles meant that there were letters from many parents on 26th January.

The Education Act of 1880, which made school attendance to the age of ten compulsory, also tried to penalise truancy by only issuing certificates if a child's attendance was up to a certain standard. This resulted in 27 parents being summoned before the magistrate for sending their children irregularly or not at all. The magistrate ordered the children to attend school. Where illness was the cause of absenteeism, no orders were given. On 23rd February the School Attendance Committee paid the fees of several children sent to school. The attendance had improved after the above summonses were issued.

On 30th March William Crookham was absent again, the reason given being that 'my brother was here so I stayed at home'.

The school was closed all day on 9th April for the West Norfolk election.

F. Green, pupil teacher, was told about boxing a boy's ears in class 5th May and again on 13th. This was not the first time this had happened and on 25th May F. Green was told yet again.

Attendances under the new Education Act improved, but in a few cases fines were imposed whenever the orders were not complied with.

On 29th May HM Inspector reported that the pupils' results were 'very fairly well' in grammar and geography.

William Crookham away with a cold, but had been seen about the town a great part of the time. He returned a week later, only to be absent again the next day without a note. Then he was away all week with a cold, but again was seen about the town. The managers gave him 6 months' notice, but Mr Pheasant asked his father to take him away before the six months if anything could be found for him. He left the school on 6th July by mutual agreement with the managers.

On 14th July the attendance was diminished owing to the labourers' demonstration headed by a brass band and the labourers carried banners. After a public tea in the White Lion clubroom, in the evening Joseph Arch, founder of the Agricultural Workers' Union, addressed a meeting in the Corn Hall.

The new curate, B. G. Smith, impressed the master by attending school every morning to take a scripture lesson from 9.15 to 9.45 and then took the second class in Scripture.

On 20th July the three Sunday schools of the non-conformists (Wesleyans, Primitive Methodists and Baptists) had a united treat. This was in connection with the centenary of the Sunday schools. Attendance that afternoon was 'thin'.

Children who attended Sunday school at the Church were given a treat on the Vicarage Field, with their parents.

1881

January 18th saw very cold weather with several inches of snow. There had been snow and severe cold with 22 degrees of frost. Strong winds blew the snow off the rooftops and formed large drifts in the road. The next day there were immense snowdrifts, stopping the trains and mail coaches. The railway men were employed the whole night clearing the snow from the cuttings. The first train from Swaffham to Lynn was snowed up for several hours in the railway cuttings. Tradesmen's carts which had gone out the previous day were stuck overnight before they could get back. The mail cart could not go to Brandon, nor Litcham or Rougham. No mail was received from London or the provinces. School attendance was small in both morning and afternoon, as it was on 24th January when there were 17 degrees of frost accompanied by fog.

February 28th was another day of heavy snow and very cold weather.

On March 1st a group of eight boys were sent from the workhouse after the Guardians had received a letter from the school managers saying that they 'would rather not receive the children, but would not refuse to do so. The payments, however, would be higher than the other children. The Education Department, on being appealed to, said that if there were room the workhouse children must be admitted. But the rate of payment might be higher than the ordinary fee.'

A new door leading from the peg house onto the Campingland started being used on 9th May.

The Government Inspector's report, received on the 15th May, referred to the difficulties encountered with an increase of children in the school. The diocesan inspector also referred to the school 'being large, but the discipline is good'.

Two assistant masters came and went within a few months. An ex-pupil teacher, J. Hare, began work as assistant master on 31st October.

1882

The schools were closed from 17th April until 22nd May by medical authority due to scarlet fever in the town.

The Foresters, including men and juveniles, celebrated their anniversary on 30th May. They attended church and paraded the town. The school had a half-day holiday in the afternoon following 'thin' attendance in the morning.

The Science and Art department held one of their frequent drawing exams on 26th June. Pupil teachers and all pupils were examined.

A steam roundabout formed a great attraction on 25th July, after the rain had fallen 'in torrents' from 12 noon until 4 p.m. The usual short church service had to be abandoned. This was the Sunday school and juvenile members of the Church of England Temperance Society. Tea was provided in the Vicarage Field and the children played until dusk.

G. Hill was absent because his boots went to be mended.

Another school treat took place on 28th September, this time with the Church of England Temperance Society.

Mr Pheasant criticised the Education authorities for not enforcing the Education Act. The officer rarely visited the school; when he did turn up, it was just to say that attendance committee was going to pay for two girls and that the headmistress be told.

Rev. Gwynne was a member of the Committee organising the 'Fine Art Exhibition' in the Assembly Rooms and was therefore absent from school on 23rd October.

Mrs Hunton came to the school to correct her son's age, incorrectly entered on the attendance register. The evidence she produced was the family Bible, with all names and dates in it. The register was corrected.

On 18th December the master commented that during the past three weeks names of the same irregular children had been sent in repeatedly. The attendance officer did not seem to take any notice of this. On 22nd December a bill was sent to the Attendance Officer for the loss of income from non-pauper children who were regular non-attenders.

1883

In January attendance was improved, not by the attendance officer looking them up but by absence inquiry forms, as recommended by HM Inspector on 30th October 1882. All the principal teachers of the Boys, Girls and Infants Schools were invited to meet the School Attendance Committee at the workhouse on 22nd January. The Absence Inquiry forms used since Christmas had done an immense amount of good. In a few cases however, parents had refused to fill them up. Yesterday an enquiry was made by the teachers in the presence of Mr Gwynne, when six children stated that when coming to school in the afternoon, Mrs Wilkinson (the Attendance Officer's wife) said that if any more papers (attendance inquiry forms) were sent to their homes, they were to burn them.

Another meeting of the Attendance Committee was held on 5th February from 12.30 to 3.15.

On 5th March the Attendance Officer (Mr Wilkinson) attended school to inquire about returns of irregular children; this was the first time this year he had been to the school. The forms were sent in with the parents' names.

From 9th to 16th March several children were away with colds and sore feet because the weather was very wintry with frequent heavy snow squalls.

A new Attendance Officer, Mr Robert Smith, who was an ex-inspector of the Metropolitan Police, started work on 2nd April.

Cases of ringworm, scarlet fever, inflammation of the lungs were all reported in the book during April. In May measles struck the children, but was not so severe in June.

HM Inspector's report, received on 26th June, said that with greater regularity of attendance, both would be excellent schools. However, the new Attendance Officer visited the school once a week, unlike his predecessor.

On 4th July the school managers decided that the children should bring their school money on the first time they come to school that week.

F. Green was absent ill according to his brother Edmund.

T. Fendick was given one month's notice in consequence of parents' complaints of him hitting boys.

A new rule came into effect on 1st October of sending children back if they arrived without their school money. A consequence of this was that the school money was paid on Monday morning.

On 26th October F. Green and T. Fendick finished at the school.

Prizes for regular and punctual attendance started being given out on 8th November. The prizes were books, 25 altogether.

Several children were away on 9th November with sore throats. There had been several deaths in the parish from croup or diphtheria.

1884

Frederick Jarmine was discharged on 24th January, having been with the school since October. The reason was irregular attendance.

On 22nd May the children were away for the homecoming of Capt. Wilson.

On 22nd July the Church Sunday school children had their treat and the day school had a holiday. The party were conveyed to Castleacre in 12 waggons and waggonettes, some of which were lent by the farmers. The children carried their flags and tea was served among the ruins at Castleacre.

School broke up for the harvest holidays on 1st August, harvest having commenced on most of the farms. With excessively hot and dry weather, the harvest had been finished for a fortnight by the time school recommenced on 8th September.

Twelve inches (30 cm) of snow fell overnight on 1st December and attendance was affected. The next day a thaw set in, and the streets were in a dreadful state.

1885

To mark the coming-of-age of Prince Albert Victor on 8th January, all the children of the boys', girls' and infants' schools were presented with a bun and an orange. During the day the bells were rung; at night there was a bonfire on the Market Place with fireworks. (Grandson of Queen Victoria, the prince was second in line of succession to the throne but died in January 1892.)

On 15th January Mr Pheasant writes that the attendance throughout the week was affected by the wintry weather. The streets were in a dreadful state during the thaw after there must have been about 18 inches (45 cm) of snow through the week.

HM Inspector conducted an examination on 16th and 17th April at which 184 boys were present. Although the Diocesan inspectors were clergymen of course, there for taking exams in scripture etc., HM Inspectors were mostly also clergy, in this case Rev. H. Smith and Mr Johnson, his assistant.

Staff on 9th June: Mr Wm Pheasant *Certificated Master, First Class*
J. R. Mottram *Assistant, Article 50*
G. V. Hooton *Assistant, Article 50*
P. Hill *Pupil Teacher, 3rd Year*
J. Fishpool *Pupil Teacher 1st Year*
E. Powley *Pupil Teacher, 1st Year*

On 11th June the Baptist Sunday school had their annual treat and were taken in waggons to Castleacre.

The Diocesan Inspector reported that the 'Swaffham boys were carefully and successfully taught'.

On 30th June the Church Sunday school children were again at Castleacre for their annual treat. They played amongst the ruins and had tea. The day was fine.

The cutting of oats commenced on 7th August and the harvest began on the Monday, except on farms where there was a strike among the labourers as to harvest wages.

On 12th September the pupil teachers and children placed in the first class in the scripture examination, went to Norwich where the Bishop of the Diocese entertained them and many others to lunch in the Palace grounds.

On 11th November children were away because Bostock & Wombwell's menagerie was in town. The 'Beast did not arrive until 1.30 p.m.'

There was a holiday on 4th December because the school was being used for polling in the election of a Member of Parliament.

1886

There was a lot of snow in January, which made the roads into a terrible state when it thawed.

Mumps was very common at the time of HM Inspector's visit on 5th and 6th April. Many children came to school for the examination with their faces wrapped up. On one or two occasions children came after being sent for, having been marked sick in the registers. In the afternoon the children had a holiday, but on 9th fresh cases of mumps were still breaking out.

G. B. Hooton left on May 3rd and the managers reduced the staff numbers, appointing a pupil teacher as assistant.

Many boys were absent on 24th June for the Baptist Sunday school treat. The choirboys went to Yarmouth for their Sunday school treat.

An entry on 3rd August records that measles was spreading through the town and that several children were away.

1887

Henry Elfleet was drowned shortly after leaving school on 25th January. With three other boys, he went to the pit in the Antinghams. He went out on to the ice, which was dangerous owing to the thaw. The ice broke and before assistance arrived he was lost. Mr Fowler, the butcher, pulled the body out of the pit with a rake. 'All efforts by Messrs Thomas & Marriot, surgeons, to restore animation, failed.'

There was a holiday on 23rd June for the Queen's (Golden) Jubilee. Celebration of the Jubilee at Cockley Cley was on another day, so many people and children from Swaffham went there.

1888

The attendance suffered on 14th February because of a snowfall overnight and during the day of about 8 inches (20 cm). This bad weather continued until 9th March, and worsened once more on 14th March. The attendance varied accordingly, but was generally quite good considering the conditions. A good many boys were away one afternoon in order to see the military funeral of Private H. G. Chittock of the Swaffham Rifle Volunteer Corps.

HM Inspector's report was received on 29th April; it said the school was continuing in a thoroughly satisfactory condition.

Necton Hall gardens were open to the public on 9th August; as a consequence, several boys were away in the afternoon.

When the school resumed on 24th September, the harvest had not been completed. The corn was in a backward state owing to the cold and wet weather. The first three weeks of the holiday were very wet in this district.

1889

HM Inspector awarded the school an Excellent Merit Grant.

A terrific storm raged overnight in the town and neighbourhood on 3rd June. The school windows of both boys' and girls' schools on the south side were a complete wreck, caused by hail stones of as much as 4.5 inches (114 mm) in circumference.

A severe tempest hit the town on 7th June, lasting from 2 a.m. to 10 a.m. A few children braved the weather, but were sent home. The school was not opened.

A Primrose fete was held at Cockley Cley on 25th July. That, and the Wesleyan Sunday school treat at Swaffham, meant that the attendance was affected. (The Primrose League was a Conservative Party organisation).

Michaelmas Day saw a few families leaving the town. This was an annual occurrence, as farm labourers would only have work for a year at a time and would be moving to another farm, sometimes in other parishes.

1890

Influenza affected the boys and the master (twice) in early 1890 for a long while.

A draft of children came from the Infants' school on 25th April; a large number of them were very backward indeed in reading.

When school began again on 2nd June, the subscriptions had fallen off considerably in late years due to deaths and removal. The remaining subscribers held a meeting in the Boys' room and the Rev. Canon Winter presided. A new committee was appointed: The Vicar, The Curate (Rev. A. A. Avan) and Messrs H.W. Day, W. H. Plowright, A. J. Winter, F. Morse, T. W. Clark and Larwood (the Pool). The committee agreed to meet again on 23rd June, but the proceedings were adjourned for a fortnight. The managers met on 30th to consider increasing the subscriptions to the schools. The Committee met again on 21st September 1891 and decided to accept the Government's offer of 10/- per head. Under the 1891 legislation elementary education was provided free. Mr Pheasant wrote, 'The schools were today declared free, the children taking their pence home again.' This was nine years before the establishment of the National Board of Education, when free public education was available to all children in England. (It was not until 1902 that free education was available at secondary level.)

On 1st December the master wrote that a boy from the school had died from typhoid fever. He added that this was the fourth member of the family to die from this complaint.

1891

Eight weeks of very severe weather caused many pupils to be away. The snow persisted from 23rd to 26th January, when a thaw set in and milder conditions prevailed.

Henry Lee Warner was a benefactor to the school, buying various items to help with education.

On 7th July, from 1.30 to 2.00, a tempest passed through the town, causing some boys to be absent.

Drawing was introduced as a new lesson on 16th July and notices given to the science department. It was found necessary to amend the timetable in order to bring this subject in, for at least an hour and a half each week.

On 1st July heavy rain fell and the weather continued in this manner for the whole of July. On 10th August the attendance was less than usual due to more rain. The school holiday did not start until 14th August (lasting until 21st September) because of the very poor conditions for harvesting.

Whooping cough was about for a while, affecting attendances. Names were being sent in for irregularity to the Attendance Officer – 21 names were sent to the Attendance Officer on 30th October for being absent twice or more during the week. This continued each week.

Assistant masters came and went with regularity. Some were taking up better positions elsewhere, others just left.

The first payment under the 1891 Free Education Act was received on 3rd December 1891, the money being for the last quarter of the year, commencing September.

Influenza caused some boys to be away sick on 22nd December.

1892

Upon returning to school after the Christmas holiday on 11th January, it was noted that there was a tremendous amount of sickness about the town. There were an estimated 300 cases in the town, over 10% of the population.

Several inches of snow fell overnight on 18th February, affecting attendance. The wintry weather over the week meant that no absenteeism reports were sent in. Severe weather continued in March affecting attendance.

The drawing exam on 15th March involved 153 boys (out of 155); the examiner was early because East Bradenham school was closed due to influenza and consequently the exam there was cancelled. The finished papers were sealed in a bag and sent to London.

A bazaar was held in the Assembly Rooms on 27th April in aid of the restoration of the church roof and warming the church. The bazaar continued the next day and in the evening of the third day.

Cases of measles were prevalent in the town by 18th May and the children of families where measles occurred were sent home. Several adults were affected, including the Vicar.

On 24th May HM Inspector's report was received and he noted that the school continued in a very satisfactory manner.

A copy of the school accounts was posted on the girls' school gate, as required by the Education Department, from 20th June until 6th July. A copy of the Inspector's report was available for inspection at the vicarage.

On 29th/30th June a terrific tempest raged the whole night, from 10 p.m. until 7 a.m. the next morning. The sky was still very black at 9 a.m. and rain was falling heavily. Attendance was less.

The fee grant of £52 10s for the past quarter was received in early July. This sum was for the Boys', Girls' and Infants' schools.

On 15th July Rev. A. A. Avan came to the school in the morning, but the attendance was less than usual, owing, no doubt, to the parliamentary election which had taken place. The candidates were Mr Hare and Mr Lee Warner.

On 18th July, attendance was less than usual, owing to the Wesleyans Sunday school treat. The children were taken by train to Hunstanton.

The attendance was greatly reduced in the afternoon of 11th August owing to a bazaar auction in the Vicarage in aid of the church roof restoration. The band of the King's Royal Irish Hussars attended. Fossell's Circus was also in the town and children were admitted at 2d each.

During the summer holiday the school's ceilings were whitened and the walls recoloured. The work was done by a Mr Heyhoe. The £25 cost included the repair of the lead and new lead in several of the windows.

The Queen's Scholarship results were announced; Ernest A. Arthurton, a pupil teacher in the school, had come number 161 in the class. He also gained a first class in the Scripture examination on the Battersea list. (He left the school on 22nd December to take up a place at St John's College, Battersea.)

A new assistant, Mr Edward Caperwell from Manchester, started on 31st October. He had failed his scholarship examination earlier in the year. Another assistant, A. M. Lack, started on 7th November on trial but left on 18th November as his discipline was so poor it was impossible to keep him.

The names of 30 children who were in the habit of being away once every week were sent in to the Attendance Officer on 18th November. The Attendance Officer came in on 21st and said he had issued warnings in all the above 30 cases. The entry for 25th November records that the cautions given had good effect during the week.

Mr Vernon Smith called at the school on 2nd December to ask about using a room at the school for art classes for members of the Young Men's Friendly Society.

A lot of snow fell overnight on 8th/9th December.

1893

Henry Grand, late assistant in Wellingborough, started on 9th January.

H. Coe was repeatedly spoken to about boxing boys' ears in school but it seemed to have no effect.

Fifty children were admitted from the Infants' School on 2nd May; HM Inspector had suggested all six-year-olds who could do their work should come. HM Inspector continued to report that the school continued in a very satisfactory condition.

On 14th June the headmaster was ordered to rest owing to serious nervous debility.

The school closed by medical authority for three weeks from 7th July because of mumps, and the harvest holiday commenced on 31st July. The school resumed under care of G. Matthews, standing in for Mr Pheasant, who was ill. Owing possibly to the eight weeks' holiday and Mr Pheasant's illness, the standard throughout the school in arithmetic had fallen. All other subjects were fairly good, but many boys were still harvesting. A half-day holiday on 21st September celebrated the Harvest Thanksgiving.

On 29th September a complaint was received regarding Mr Caperwell striking a boy. He was cautioned about this, but on 7th December another complaint was received and Mr Caperwell was again warned.

On 3rd October, three boys and a master were suffering from scarlet fever, and on the following day another two were ill with it. Ten days later, 14 were absent suffering from scarlet fever. The fever spread, and on 17th Mr Matthews recorded that 22 boys were away, either suffering from it, or having it in the house. Four boys from the workhouse were not permitted to attend school according to Medical Officer's instructions. By 27th, some 30 boys out of a total of 190 on the books were away ill, mainly due to the fever.

On 10th November, Dr Thomas (Medical Officer) told Mr Matthews that he intended to close the school because of the prevalence of fever. A week later, though, it was reported that the school would not close. The fever gradually diminished.

1894

It was not until 8th January that Mr Pheasant returned to his duties, but the doctor had recommended that he did not attempt too much at first, so Mr Matthews stayed on.

On 26th January, Mr Pheasant examined standards 1 and 2 in arithmetic. It is recorded that 'several boys in Standard 2 (teacher Mr Caperwell) instead of doing their sums, put down any figures'.

On 12th February Mr Henry Grand, assistant, left without informing the managers. He had obtained a better position under the Nottingham School Board. He was replaced on the 13th February by Mr W. Pleasance, who was however obliged to return home, being diagnosed as severely ill.

E. Caperwell's class was examined and found to be wanting. Sums were difficult and dictation was poor on 27th February.

An improvement had been noticed in the attendance of 13 boys who had been away at least once a week and whose parents the Attendance Officer had cautioned.

G. F. Sporne's class was regularly tested and found to be behind other classes. He was spoken to about boxing a boy's ears, and then Mr Caperwell was spoken to for knocking a boy about the head with a book. Mr Sporne left the school on 3rd April.

The Attendance Officer dealt with several boys for habitual absenteeism and a very great improvement was noted.

A meeting was held of subscribers to the school and others interested in supporting the voluntary system, the object being to raise funds for cloakrooms, closets and a staircase at the girls' school. A good start was made and by 3rd May a meeting of the school building committee recorded that £245 out of the £280 required was promised. The committee agreed to proceed with the work as soon as the conveyancing of the land was sufficiently advanced to warrant them beginning.

On 23rd April 54 children was sent from the Infants' school, but 14 were sent back to the Infants' school as they only just knew their letters. Those taken in were backward.

On 4th May, the work of the second standard had been so poor that the managers gave the teacher, E. Caperwell, notice to leave.

Because the defects pointed out the previous year had not been put into effect, the HM Inspector reported that there was hesitation in awarding a grant this year. The managers were called upon to effect the changes as early as possible. (The erection of the new closets and other outbuildings required by the Education Committee commenced on 19th June.) HM Inspector paid a surprise visit to the school on the afternoon of 26th June but the new closets and cloakrooms had not been finished when the school resumed after the summer holidays.

Two new teachers started, but these were ladies – the first lady teachers in the boys' school – on 13th September. They were to teach Standards 1 and 2.

Measles began spreading through the school on 8th October. A large number of the younger children were affected. Dr Thomas said the outbreak was of a very sudden nature. About 80 boys were away owing to measles on 17th October. The schools were closed on the following day by medical authority. About 300 children were away in all the schools, either with measles or owing to them. (On 18th October there was published a pamphlet by Henry Lee Warner entitled *A Few Words to the Inhabitants of Swaffham*, in which he stated that the Local Government Board held the Swaffham Board responsible for zymotic diseases which were rarely absent from the town due to defective and leaking drains which had not been cemented properly when they were installed in 1871.) The epidemic was almost over when the schools resumed after about 4½ weeks. Nearly every child in the town had had measles by 19th November and two families were still affected.

One of the new lady assistants left because her work was unsatisfactory. She was replaced by a lady from the infants' school, with several years' experience.

1895

The first week of January was very wintry with snow drifts of as much as 6 feet (1.83 m) in depth. Much of the snow remained when the school reassembled after Christmas holiday. The attendance was 'pretty good' on 10th, despite the weather being 'exceedingly severe, with snow and frost' during the week. No attendance returns were sent in because of the severe weather. Free breakfasts at the Coffee Tavern during the severe weather were given to a number of poor children on five mornings per week. The vicar announced this in the morning and a list was prepared of children who would probably be glad of such breakfasts. Knee-deep snow was recorded on 28th January, after snow had fallen almost non-stop. The attendance was less. On 1st February still no attendance returns were sent in due to the very severe weather, which was so cold on the night of 6th February that 28 degrees of frost were registered at the school. Colds and chilblains kept children away during this bad weather. The Soup Distribution Committee provided a pint of hot soup on Tuesdays and Thursdays during the bad weather. Country children benefited from this.

On 27th February the choirboys were away early attending the funeral of Miss Augusta Day.

There was a 'terrific hurricane' in the afternoon of 25th March, causing an immense amount of damage in the town. The schools had some slate blown away, but did not sustain much damage.

The children from the workhouse were kept away from school, even when there were only slight showers. This had been the case ever since they attended this school.

The HM Inspector's report received on 29th May was not as praiseworthy as before, criticising the slightly backward nature of the school, due to sickness and the bad weather. 'Falling off a little' is the phrase used in the report.

Attendance Record Books were begun in the school on 30th July.

Mr Day held a garden party for the members of the church choir and a large number of people in the town. The choirboys, or most of them, were away for the afternoon.

Miss Emily Spencer gave notice to leave on 9th September, as she was about to be married. (Married women were not expected to work at this time.)

Several children left because of the father changing jobs at Michaelmas, but five new boys were admitted who had moved into town.

Staff at 18th October:

Mr W. M. Pheasant *Master*

L. W. Bunting *Assistant*

M. A. Wright *Assistant mistress*

Emily Spencer *Assistant teacher*

Horace W. Coe *Pupil teacher of third year*

W. P. Coe *Pupil teacher of first year*

This staff list is for the boys only and they were only on the ground floor and pupil numbers were around the 200+ mark and one wonders how so many children were packed into the one building.

The names of ten children who were absent that day and the previous day employed by Mr Cooper in brushing (beating for shooting parties) at Cley were sent to the attendance officer. None of these children were qualified to absent themselves to go to work. The attendance officer came to the school because of this report and he came back on the 22nd November to report that the brushing at Cley had been put a stop to and the matter was to be brought to the attendance committee on the following Monday. The committee directed the clerk to write to Mr Cooper at Cockley Cley Hall calling his attention to the matter.

1896

On 7th February a circular from the Education Department directed that grammar or some other lesson should replace the crayon drawing lesson on Friday afternoon.

The twelve workhouse children (boys, girls and infants) were away on 18th March because it rained almost all day. These children were away when there was even a shower, Mr. Pheasant wrote, yet the country children all attended at the Boys' and Girls' Schools both morning and afternoon despite many of them travelling long distances.

H. Lee Warner offered a scholarship at Swaffham Grammar School. Notice had not been given until 7th May of the scholarship. Seven boys competed for it on 11th and the results were known on the 13th: Luther Layern won it and Frank Green of the Nursery was second.

The government report received on 5th June said that the school was 'in an efficient condition and under good discipline. The work is methodically arranged and effectively carried out.'

Horace Coe qualified under articles 50 and 52 of the Code; he consequently became a member of the staff as an assistant. He went with Mr Bunting and the choir to take part in the celebration of the 800th anniversary of Norwich Cathedral on 2nd July.

The Baptists' Sunday school treat on 23rd July took the children attending to Castleacre in waggons once more; on 30th July the Church Sunday school treat was noted. In this month, too, the town celebrated the Diamond Jubilee of Queen Victoria.

Thirty boys joined the new 'Penny Bank' started by Mr Barry on 7th September.

The making out and sending of attendance returns seemed a waste of time, as the master sent in the names of 17 boys who were absent and showed the weekly returns to the Attendance Officer but was told that though boys were habitually absent once a week 'the Committee took no notice whatever'. Of the absentees on one day, two were reported as being at work.

Bostock and Wombwell's Menagerie was in town on 5th November and Mr Pheasant and Miss Wright took 87 boys there. They were charged 3d each.

W. P. Coe, who was regularly marked as being late for lessons at 7 a.m., attended the examination of Pupil Teachers in Kings Lynn in October and passed well.

1897

The school resumed after the Christmas Holiday on 11th January.

Henry Lee Warner provided land for the boys to make nine gardens. He visited the school with the vicar on 29th January to announce this and the

rules drawn up were read to the school. The boys would go twice a week at
3.35 p.m. for an hour and a quarter's instruction by Mr Warner's gardener and
each boy grew a little of most vegetables, keeping the produce for himself. The
Education Department sanctioned the arrangement, which did not disturb the
ordinary curriculum of the school.

W. P. Coe caused Mr Pheasant 'immense trouble' with the private homework
set for him as a pupil teacher. Time after time he was late for lessons in the
morning.

'The school continues to be well taught and disciplined' according to
the report from HM Inspector received on 20th May. This is a feature of Mr
Pheasant's time as head. Not only did he care for the school well; he also was a
considerable writer in the log books. This shows up in his meticulous reporting
of every time W. P. Coe was late and sometimes a mention of the lessons set
him (Euclid, map and recitation). Absenteeism is often accounted for by a fair
being in town, especially when, as on 24th May, a circus made 'a low charge'
for admission.

The Diamond Jubilee of Queen Victoria's accession to the throne was
marked by a week's holiday at her wish.

A member of the Band of Hope Union gave a lecture against the dangers
of alcohol and temperance on 4th October. The lecturer had written that such
lectures were allowed by the Education Department in school hours, provided
an entry was written in the log book.

On 19th November new maps were obtained with the help of a special aid
grant under the new Education Act.

The Aid Grant for the Boys', Girls' and Infants' schools this year was £120
for the 'purpose of providing additional staff and apparatus and making the
deficit, which would otherwise necessarily be incurred in maintaining the
efficiency of the school, & my Lords will require to be satisfied that it has been
so expended'. The circular directed that the above be at once noted in the log
book.

1898

A mild form of influenza caused many children to be away in January. There
was a considerable amount of sickness in the town, including the headmaster.

A letter was received from the Headmaster of the Swaffham Grammar
School (Mr Humphries) to the effect that an old pupil of the school, Luther
Layern, was the only student in East Anglia to achieve First Class Honours in

the 2,500 candidates and 65 First Class. He was also on the Special Distinction list for Euclid. To commemorate this, the next day the boys had a holiday.

W. P. Coe was repeatedly told off for being late in the mornings and not looking after his class (the First Standard) adequately. The managers gave him notice to leave immediately after his apprenticeship ended on 31st March.

Two scholarships at Swaffham Grammar School were competed for on 26th April; one was a free one, the other given by the vicar. The event was conducted in the Vicarage Rooms by Mr H. Lee Warner and 23 boys competed. Norman Layern and Bernard Coe were successful.

The HMI report received on 16th May commented that the work was going on quietly and well in most classes.

W. P. Coe obtained a First Class pass in the Queen's Scholarship Examination (possibly to the surprise of Mr Pheasant).

In the *Norwich Mercury* of Saturday 4th June, there is a reference to the Sunday school Anniversary of the Primitive Methodists. 'On Monday the children had their annual treat in a meadow lent by Mr Larwood. A public tea was provided, to which a goodly number sat down.' Mr Pheasant, as usual, had to record the reduction in attendance that afternoon.

Mr Pheasant recorded on 12th September that the Education Act had been suspended and that suspension did not expire until Saturday 17th September. He did not send any returns of absentees until the 23rd, when 14 names were sent in for irregularity. It is likely that the suspension was to enable boys to be away from school to help with the harvest.

Registers were examined regularly and the log books signed by one of the School Governors. On 5th October, Septimus Barry 'examined the registers and found them correct'.

A menagerie circus was performing in the town on the afternoon of 16th November, consequently only one half of the children were at school. Mr Johnson, assistant to HM Inspector, examined the children on 25th.

The 26th Annual Congress of the General Association of Church School Managers and Teachers was held in Norwich in 1898 and was reported in the *Norwich Mercury*. The objects of the association were:

> **First, to bring Church school managers and teachers into closer union, for the purpose of enabling them to give expression to their opinions on any public question affecting national education.**
>
> **Second, to protect the liberty of religious teaching in Church**

schools, and to enable managers and teachers to lend their combined influence to secure its efficiency.

Third, to enable managers and teachers to exert their due influence in the protection of the many important interests common to both, which are seriously affected from time to time by the regulations of the Council Office, and other causes.

Dean Lefroy, of Norwich, said he was not jealous of 'the advances made by the School Board system, and he could not understand why there could not be a kindlier feeling between these two contingents of the educational army.'

Problems with funding Church schools were a feature of this meeting. Run by the Church with a state grant, plus diminishing voluntary subscriptions, it was a continual struggle to keep up with the demands of an ever-growing educational system. There was a resistance to giving up control of the schools, but an agreement to allow other bodies to be represented on the management. There was a fear that by giving up control, religious teaching would be stopped.

Mr Gray, MP, said there was 'violent antagonism to one system and a denial of all the defects of the other'. He said that there were defects in the two systems, but some of the best schools in the country were voluntary. In rural districts the question of school buildings, staff and management caused problems.

THE PROPOSED SCHOOL BOARD ✠ (or BOARD SCHOOL?

Top of poster (Swaffham Museum)

Space had been found in schools for every child, but they (government) had not found the means to make every school space healthy. The inferiority of the Church school staff compared with Board schools was evident in the staff qualifications, where a large number of people were employed with no technical qualifications because they were cheap – £30–£40 per year.

Referring to the fall in the number of subscribers, Mr Gray said that National schools should not be dependent on local charity. The government should fund the whole cost of maintenance of all public elementary schools. This would entail the taking over of all schools and a county Board of Education to control primary and secondary education. Religious teaching should be a reality and not a sham, with a view to the Diocesan Inspector's visit and his 'over-estimated report'.

The congress closed after a series of motions, which could be summarised in part of one motion – 'the cost of maintenance of secular education should be defrayed out of national taxation'.

1899

Topham Cutforth began work as an assistant.

Whooping cough was prevalent on 19th January and children from families with whooping cough in the home were prevented from coming to school, by order of the Medical Officer of Health. Despite this measure, on 3rd March there was still a great deal of whooping cough and sickness in the town, but some few had returned to school.

On 8th March, a poll of ratepayers was taken at the Shirehall with reference to Mr Lee Warner's proposal for the establishment of a School Board and Board Schools in the town. (School Boards were not under the control of the Church. 'Distinctive religious teaching' was not allowed in Board Schools.) The agitation has been going on since 21st November 1898.

The arguments that followed are mostly financial, but paragraph 3 is interesting:

> **A School Board may consist of and may employ as teachers – Roman Catholics, or persons of any belief or none, Atheists or Infidels. In the present school the teachers from outside Swaffham are Church people; but Nonconformists living in Swaffham have been, and are employed, as teachers, without any distinction.**

The poster ends: 'We therefore earnestly hope that for the SAKE of JUSTICE, and for the SAKE of the CHILDREN'S HIGHEST GOOD, YOU WILL VOTE AGAINST Either a Board School or a School Board.' (One of the main arguments for Board Schools was the unfair influence of subscribers in the National Schools.) However, the voting for a Board was 153, against 435.

In the evening of 14th April there was a meeting of the Church Temperance Society for the boys belonging to it. In the morning several inkstands had been overturned and the ink had been emptied under the desk in the place for slates etc.

HM Inspector's report included the fact that the boys were being well taught, but the rooms for the boys were inconveniently full for teaching purposes.

In June, Mr Cutforth was ill and the managers decided his illness was not appropriate for a teacher. He left on 8th June.

Mr Harrison, an official of the Great Eastern Railway, visited the school on 23rd June as his company had been approached for assistance in the building of a new school.

On 4th July the church choirboys were absent owing to them playing a cricket match against Narborough church choirboys.

The schools were closed in the afternoon of 6th July owing to the Church Sunday school treat.

On 3rd August many boys were away because Manlay's Circus was in town and giving a cheap performance.

In the afternoon of 16th October, all the boys, together with the girls and infants, attended the laying of the foundation stone of the new Girls' School by the Honourable Miss Margaret Amherst. The registers were not marked.

D. Thomas, the Medical Officer of Health, attended school on 17th November to inquire as if there were any cases of mumps in the school. All those affected by having mumps in the house were excluded. This did not stop the illness spreading, because by 20th November mumps seems to be spreading rapidly and intrusively. (It was thought to be connected with the damp and foggy weather, and on 15th December the school was closed by the Medical Officer of Health.)

Eleven boys were examined on 30th November for a free scholarship at the Grammar School. The exam took place in the Vicarage Rooms under Mr H. Lee Warner.

1900

Influenza was prevalent in the town in January and many children were away with mumps, sore faces and influenza throughout January and for much of February.

The new curate, Rev. C. L. Norriss, attended school for the first time on 24th January. The vicar gave a talk on the war with the Boers on 8th February.

Due to the weather, the boys were not able to work on their garden; by 14th March additional lessons were necessary.

A bazaar was held to raise funds for the building fund for the new Girls'

School and alterations to the Boys' School.

On 2nd May, military drill was introduced into the timetable, with Sgt Instructor Brewster drilling the boys. A meeting held on 4th May discussed military drill and the furnishing of the new Girls' School.

HM Inspector called on 17th May and reported that the school was being very well taught and could claim an additional grant in respect of this. Some of the elder boys were doing well in the garden, and the Inspector asked for medical certificates.

When school began again on 11th June, the girls had moved to their new school and the boys were able to use both floors of the old school.

Five boys were away with typhoid fever in their houses on 21st June.

The boys, the headmaster and the teachers went to a missionary exhibition in connection with the Society for the Propagation of the Gospel in the Assembly Rooms on 19th July. Many articles from foreign lands were shown and addresses given by different gentlemen.

The circus was in town again on 23rd July caused attendances to be less in the afternoon because the parents of the boys allowed this.

Sgt Brewster was away from the school from the 18th July until after the harvest holidays, owing to the fact that he was at a volunteer encampment at Colchester. The alterations to the school continued after the school holidays, disrupting lessons.

The school was closed in the afternoon of 18th October to enable the children to attend the reopening of the church bells at the expense of Mrs Day in Memory of H. W. Day, one of the school managers.

Bostock & Wombwell's menagerie visited the town on 14th November. At 3.30 some 92 boys, plus three teachers, left the school and paid 2d. each admission.

November saw unusually high rainfall. Several children were away with colds and sore throats.

1901

Mrs Pheasant, who had resigned her position as head of the Girls' School, took charge of standard four and the two upper rooms under her husband's supervision on 7th January.

On 29th January Charles Copsey found half a sovereign in Church Lane and handed it to the Headmaster, who made enquiries as to the loss of the coin, but with no result. The head subsequently sent the coin in a note to the boy's mother.

On Tuesday morning 12th February the headmaster showed the school the special editions of *The Sphere* and *Illustrated London News* showing funeral pictures of Queen Victoria.

Mr Pheasant was strict with one of the teachers regarding her methods of dictation, reprimanding her and telling her that the lesson would be stopped if it happened again. The same teacher as in trouble again on 22nd March for dictating words in individual syllables.

Attendance prizes of one cricket ball and three cricket bats were awarded to four boys who had not been absent all the year ending 31st March.

In June the HMI report was not as good as previous years, reference being made to discipline problems in some parts.

The boys were unable to plant seedlings in their garden plots because of the prolonged drought, Mr Hudson the instructor reported on 26th June. However, prizes for the best cultivated gardens were distributed at The Paddocks by Mrs Lee Warner on 12th July 12th. The first prize was five shillings and the second prize was half a crown.

The Baptist and Wesleyan Sunday schools combined to provide a treat on the afternoon of 4th July, so attendance at school was less. A lecture on varied occupations was given on the following afternoon. Subjects included basket making, cutting fretwork patterns, the making of picture frames and articles of furniture and copying pictures etc.

There was a holiday in the afternoon of the 18th July for the Church Sunday school treats.

Since before Christmas, the ink supplied by Mr Coe had been of very bad quality and the ink drops from the pens formed something like grease spots. The head had made frequent complaints to him.

The results of the examination of the various standards were hung up.

The Church organ was reopened in the afternoon of 19th September, having undergone alterations and repairs.

Attendance was low in the afternoon of 30th September owing to a circus in town. Another circus was in town on 3rd October and in the afternoon so few boys attended school it was thought advisable not to open.

The boys were using 'new copy books' in October but the standard had declined in 5, 6 and 7 owing to Mr Mitchell taking singing upstairs. The slates seemed to have disappeared.

The aid grant for the school totalled £150 for 1901 and covered teaching and equipment such as apparatus, books and repair of furniture.

On 22nd October a scholarship examination took place to determine who, out of four boys, was to be allowed to go to the Grammar School. This was won by Lawrence Coe.

Measles broke out in the town on the 20th November and several boys were away with the complaint. Illness seemed to be spreading amongst the little boys; several had measles. It spread in early December in the 1st and 4th Standards. Examinations were cancelled for these standards because of the measles. The number of children attending was less every day.

1902

School opened on 6th January but was closed before 11 a.m. under the orders of Dr Thomas for two weeks, because of the measles. This made three weeks, plus Christmas Holidays, that the school was closed due to this. There was very thin attendance on 31st January due to very heavy snow and measles.

The HM Inspector reported that the ground floor classroom was 'imperfectly warmed' and needed to be properly warmed under the Education Act.

Scarletina was about the town on 26th May, as well as measles.

On Monday morning 2nd June, news came that peace had been proclaimed with the Boers; in the afternoon, children were given a holiday.

There was a difference of 55 between the attendance in the morning of 12th June and the afternoon, due to the combined Sunday school treats of the Baptists and Wesleyans.

18th June the wet, wintry weather prevented the boys from attending their garden plots after 10th June and the afternoon of 18th was the next time they could go.

The King expressed a desire that all schools should have a week's holiday to celebrate the Coronation.

Chicken pox was in the town and Dr Thomas once again visited the school and excluded from school those who had chicken pox or measles in their houses.

On 6th August, Messrs Toogood & Sons of Southampton gave prizes for the best bunch of flowers grown by the boys in the gardens at Mr Lee Warner's. A bronze medal and two certificates were given. Mr and Mrs J. H. Turner judged the flowers. George Ward won the bronze medal, and certificates went to Leicester Young, Robert Reynolds and Harold Buck.

Mrs Pheasant was away, being seriously ill.

School began again on 15th September, but due to the bad weather and heavy rain during the last five weeks, the harvest was far from over. The

Elementary Education Act was suspended, thus permitting child labour until Monday 22nd September. A good many children were still employed in the cornfields.

On 16th September Miss Wright was absent due to illness. This is a frequent entry. This time the journey from Lincoln to Swaffham had upset her; she was away for a fortnight.

Bostock & Wombwell's menagerie came again and 117 boys and three teachers went, paying 2d each. Lessons continued until 4.15 for the 51 boys who did not have the money.

On 4th December 4th HMI examined Leicester Young and questioned him, as he was the only candidate for a free scholarship at Swaffham Grammar School.

The severe winter weather meant that several children were away with colds, sore throats, chilblains, etc.

1903

Whooping cough spread through the town during January and February but the schools stayed open.

The boys commenced gardening on 24th February.

The Society for Prevention of Cruelty to Children held a meeting in the Assembly Rooms. School closed early to enable teachers to attend. The meeting was at the invitation of Mr & Mrs Lee Warner.

Mrs Pheasant was away ill for some time – 15th April to 8th June.

On 4th May HMI's report was favourable as usual with some subjects getting a better comment than others. The boys were said to be 'on the whole, well advanced'.

Norfolk County Council asked for an inventory of the school contents on 22nd May, and the list is as follows:

FURNITURE

DESKS	30 each	10 feet long
	3	9½ " "
	8	9 " "
	3	8 " "
	4	7 " "

Chairs 2, Forms 5, stools 8, Harmonium 1, Teachers' desks 3,

Wall clocks 4, Boxes 6, Small tables 6, large tables 2, show cases 2 (cotton & mustard etc.), Notice-boards 3, Fenders 2, Coal Scuttles 2, Pokers 3, tongs 3, Fireguards, 4, Dustpans 2, blinds 16, hassocks 8, cupboards large 6, small 4.

APPARATUS
Maps 24, pictures 41, easels 6, blackboards 7, Bacon's Geographical Pictures 12, Bacon's drawing charts 4, Tonic Sol-Fa Charts 5, conscience clauses 2, table and figure charts 5, drawing models 1 set, Framed slates 169, Drawing slates 33.

BOOKS

Bibles		92 copies
Royal Atlas Reader	Book 6	57
Royal	5	51
Royal	4	53
Royal	3	40
Chamber's 20th Century Reader 5		50
Whitehall Annals of England (Std 5)		70
Whitehall Sketches of English History		36
Blackwood's Geographical Reader 6		45
The World at Home	Standard 6	43
'Masterman Ready'		60
Stories from English History		34
Arnold's Object Readers Book 3		35
Arnold's	2	42
Arnold's	1	41
Longman's New Reader No. 2		29
Blackie's 1st Reader		38
Viaduct Historical Reader	2	49
Viaduct	1	37

Mr Lee Warner came to the school on the morning of 8th June with Mr Bushell, the secretary recently appointed by the NCC to carry out the controversial new Education Act.

A farmer (Mr Sharp) at the Pool had been employing an 8-year-old boy to lead horses. The boy should have been at school and was reported to the Attendance Officer on 26th June.

A surveyor and his assistant from the Norfolk County Council visited the school, as all schools were being inspected prior to them being taken over under the new Education Act.

On 20th July Mr Larwood, farmer at the Grange Farm, was reported for employing his son on the farm and on 5th August at the Petty Sessions he was fined 21 shillings including costs. John Perkins, gang master of Lynn Street, was fined a similar sum for a similar offence.

The schools were taken over by the Norfolk County Council on 30th September.

On 9th October a stock book was received from the NCC, but no attendance forms. A rough list of irregular attendees was sent to the Attendance Officer. The first supply of forms arrived a week later.

On 5th November attendance was low due to a circus in town and a hare-coursing meeting.

Miss Annie Constance Robinson began work on 5th October, but left on 16th November having represented herself as a teacher under Article 68 though she had simply been a paid monitoress at a previous school for eight weeks. She should have started on 26th September, but sent a telegram and letter saying she had met with a bad bicycle accident, but in truth she had not had an accident, nor had she owned a bicycle. She told the mistress at her previous school that she had to leave because 'her lover, to whom she was to be married next spring, had been killed the previous day by a fall from his horse in Liverpool.' The whole tale was false.

There were 180 boys on the books on 16th November; 166 boys were present when the school attendance officer called about cases of sickness.

Winter illnesses began to show. Colds and sore throats were attributed to the long spell of damp weather. Measles also began to reappear, with one or two reported cases, chiefly amongst the younger boys.

On 27th November, the attendance having been over 90% the previous seven weeks, a half-holiday was given in accordance with the recommendation of the Norfolk Education Committee.

1904

The Boys' school was divided into two parts, with standards 1, 2 and 3 upstairs, under a mistress, and 4, 5, 6 and 7 downstairs, under Mr and Mrs Pheasant. The desks in the main room were entirely rearranged into two groups of seven each. However, the work of the school was carried on with very great difficulty due to this rearrangement.

H. Lee Warner invited the garden boys to tea at the Paddocks on 14th January.

The Chairman of the governors of the Grammar School, Mr T. A. H. Hamond, came to the school on 14th January, about the free scholarship to the school.

A question arose as to the ownership of the harmoniums in the Boys' and Girls' Schools. The question was whether the day or Sunday schools owned them, but the harmoniums were part of a legacy left to the National schools.

Leaflets for distribution to all parents of boys in standards 5, 6 and 7 about two free scholarships to the grammar school for three years were brought into school by one of the school managers. Twelve boys took the examination on 30th January. Horace Wheeler and Cecil Dillistone were the successful candidates.

Another half-day holiday was granted on 26th February, as the boys had made 90% attendance during the four weeks after the Christmas holidays.

In March the gardening class re-started, six boys having left and six boys replaced them.

On 25th March the attendance officer reported that two boys were singing at a Wesleyan sale of work. This attendance officer became a more frequent visitor to the school, as a consequence of his attention to his duties; absenteeism showed a marked decline. The headmaster noted that the officer had been 'very good at looking up boys'.

Thirty boys (standard 3) came from the junior boys' department (upstairs) to form the new standard 4 after the Easter holidays.

A labour examination was held on Saturday 9th April, when 26 boys and girls were present from the various schools in the town and neighbourhood.

On the Friday afternoon a holiday was given as the percentage of attendance was over 90% for the past month.

On 19th and 21st April every boy on the registers was present. This was the first time such a high attendance had been recorded over a period of time. An all-time high of 97% attendance at school for a whole month was rewarded with a Friday afternoon holiday.

The Swaffham Fair in May had gone down considerably. Formerly the Market Place had been crowded with cattle, sheep, shows and stalls, but this year it was not thought necessary to give a holiday to the children. Attendance was good at school.

Mrs Pheasant and Mr Pheasant had collected enough money to buy for the schools two excellent sets of cricket 'things' and two sets of rounders on 16th May.

A harmonium presented to the Sunday school by Miss Kate Wilson was sent to the senior boys' school for use there. The harmonium purchased with a legacy left to the National Schools by Miss Dolignon was sent to the junior department.

On 2nd June the HMI report said that the work was going on well, although the boys in the first class 'should be stimulated to greater concentration of thought and greater earnestness in their studies'.

When Dr Thomas called on 20th June, to ask about cases of ringworm or measles in the school, he was told there was none. Every boy on the registers was present.

On 8th July the attendance reached 98.7% for the whole school; standards 4 and 5 had each reached 100%. The high attendance continued and on 15th July when Dr Thomas again called to ask about ringworm, which had appeared in the junior department, the boys had attained 96.3% and had a half-day's holiday.

When the assistant Inspector to the Norfolk Education Committee called, he left instructions that registers should be marked at 9.00 a.m., before religious instruction, instead of 9.45 when R.I. concluded. Latecomers should be marked in red when the registers were closed at 9.55 a.m. This plan was adopted from 9th September.

There was another holiday on 13th October because of high attendances (100% in two standards).

Judge Willis (of the Norfolk County Courts), passed along the Campingland one afternoon while the boys were out at play. His Honour complimented Mrs Pheasant and the master on the appearance of the boys and the manner in which they played their games.

The Education Committee allowed ten shillings for prizes for boys who had gardens. The judge was Mr. T. Green, The Nursery, Swaffham. The first prize of five shillings was awarded to V. Chamberlin, the second of half a crown to Robert Oxborough and the third prize, also half a crown, went to Alfred Brewster.

On 4th November attendance was only 92.1% owing to several boys being away ill.

An Examination for Labour Certificates was held at the school, including 28 boys from Swaffham, Oxborough, Narborough, Cressingham, Castleacre, etc. Ten boys were presented from Swaffham (standard 5) and all of them passed.

On 14th November Bostock & Wombwell's menagerie was in town again, and boys went on payment of 2d. each.

The copy of the HMI report received on 6th December was not so praiseworthy this year. The general tone of the report was that the boys 'could do better'. This is to be explained by the ill-health of both teachers.

On 7th December there was a day's holiday because the attendance was over 97% during October and November, standard 5 being 100%.

On 22nd December Mr and Mrs Pheasant retired after being connected with these schools for 41 and 42 years respectively.

1905

School reopened on 9th January after the Christmas break. Mr Horace Coe commenced duties as headmaster, the Senior and Junior departments becoming one school. Pupils on roll – 156 (from Standard 1 to standard 7). Assistant staff were Mary Anne Wright (article 52) and Florence Wright (article 50). The next day Miss Payne (ex-PT) joined from the Infants school to take standard 1 until further notice.

Mr Blockley (a correspondent) as usual collected the money for the Penny Bank on 16th January.

The result of the exam for the governors' scholarship was that Fred Banner came first.

The attendance figure (during a period of sickness in the town) was 96.6%. For the whole of January it exceeded 90%.

H. Larwood obtained a scholarship to the grammar school.

Mr Coe was very disparaging about the standard of some aspects of the teaching, criticising particularly 4 & 7 in arithmetic. He also introduced the tonic solfa method of singing. Geometry had not been taught during the past year, nor yet had physical drill. In standards 5 and 7 he found the arithmetic very weak. Apparently, no attempt had been made to teach model drawing or geometry during the past year.

Mr Lee Warner, as Chairman of the Norfolk Education Committee, visited on 14th February and was told that a male teacher was preferable for standard 3.

Mr and Mrs Pheasant were presented with a testimonial and a purse for their work in the school.

A former pupil photographed the various classes.

Another half day holiday was awarded for over 90% attendance during the month of February, usually a time of absenteeism.

Two new sets of stock arrived on 30th March and among the items were two setsquares 45° and 60° for the teachers, 4 dozen setsquares 45° for scholars and three copies of *Notes on the Metric System* (probably the 16-page booklet of that title by George Collar, published by Macmillan in 1892).

A former pupil teacher, E. V. Powley, returned to the school.

One 3rd May fifteen boys of the first class were punished with one stroke for inattention. A couple of days later, a complaint was made to the Chairman of Managers by Mr Poulsey of Ash Close that his son had been punished. The head attended a managers' meeting on 12th May in connection with Poulsey's complaint.

The attendance for April exceed 98% and a half day holiday was given.

The first annual distribution of prizes took place on 7th June at 3 p.m. The boys all assembled in the lower room. A. Brewster, H. Layern and E. Layern were amongst the boys winning medals. P. Hunn was another medal winner; he was remembered as a local postman for many years.

Another half-day holiday was given on 8th June for 97.8% attendance.

HM Inspector visited the school and examined the boys' gardens, which he said were being tended 'excellently well'.

Whooping cough was prevalent in school later in June.

On 1st July the Vicar, by direction of the managers, brought a note saying the summer holidays would be from 4th August to Monday 11th September (thus still tying the school holiday in with the harvest).

An HMI report stated that Mr Coe had the school well in hand.

Miss Ursula Vincent started work on 11th September. On the evening of 12th she expressed dissatisfaction at her inability to maintain discipline. Two days later a note was received from Miss Vincent saying she would be leaving, as she was deaf, which was all against the maintaining of discipline.

Prizes for gardening (vegetables and flowers) were given to Percy Cross, H. Howard, H. Layern and others on 15th September.

One teacher and several children were away because of extremely heavy rain.

On the centenary of the Battle of Trafalgar a ceremony took place on the Campingland at 12 o'clock. Miss K. Wilson unfurled a flag that had been presented by a gentleman of the town while the boys, teachers and managers subscribed for the socket. Both the boys and the girls sang patriotic songs.

On 7th November Mr L. Brain, Council Inspector, visited the school and condemned the desks used in the upstairs and said that the seats in the adjoining room must be altered.

A fire was caused by a boy throwing a lighted match in the air from the Pightle. It lodged in a curtain in the school. Some boys seeing smoke had the presence of mind to fetch the key and pulled the curtain down, thus preventing any damage beyond that to the curtain. It was decided at a meeting of the managers to reward those boys who had assisted in preventing a serious fire. At that same meeting, on 13th November, it was resolved that the schools should henceforth be called the 'Swaffham Church of England Schools'.

The school maintained a good attendance record, a half day holiday being given each month for attendances over 90% for a considerable time.

1906

On 13th February HM Inspector noted that the ventilation in the lower classroom was imperfect. This was remedied within a week.

On 2nd April there were 177 boys on the books and the teaching staff were Horace W. Coe (Head Teacher Cert. 1st Class), Arthur R. East, Charles C. Bush, Florence A. Lane, Mary A. Wright and Edward B. Powley (pupil teacher), giving an average class size of 35.4.

Two boys left school on 4th May because their family was emigrating to Canada.

In the first week of April there was 98.4% attendance; a holiday was given for good attendance in March, and on 19th April when Miss E. Winter of Lydney House married Mr W. Martin. The spring weather must have contributed to an attendance of 99% for the week ending 20th April. This was exceeded on 24th, when every one of the 178 boys on the registers was present.

At 3 p.m. on 24th May all the elementary schools proceeded to the Market Place for awards for good attendance. Hymns and the vicar speaking on the British Empire accompanied the proceedings. More songs and speeches followed amongst the presentations of medals and awards. In the Boys' School 43 medals were awarded and 87 prizes and certificates.

On 17th July, one boy was sent home for not having a handkerchief – he was constantly without one. As he did not return, another boy was sent for him and was told that as he was sent home, he would not be allowed to return that morning, but he would come in the afternoon.

On 20th July, the attendance of 92.5% was the lowest for eighteen months.

School was dismissed early, at 3.45 p.m., on 25th July for the Horticultural and Poultry Show.

Four boys had gone to Canada by the beginning of the new school year on 14th September. Four other boys had left too.

After a visit from the County Inspector, Mr T. A. Cox, in the company of F. M. Blockley of the school managers, the managers were informed that new desks were needed for the boys. Otherwise, the Inspector was satisfied with what he saw.

Garden prizes were still being given annually.

Staff on 22nd October were Horace Coe (Head Teacher); Mr A. R. East (certificated) and Mr E. V. Powley, Miss F. Lane and Miss M. Wright (all uncertificated). C. Parkinson, HM Inspector, said he was satisfied that the work was going very nicely; he was sorry to see so many big boys in Standard One, but knew that it was unavoidable as the boys came to school exceptionally backward, having been to school very seldom.

An epidemic of sore throats was the cause of the attendance dropping to 95.6% on 23rd November.

1907

Eight new desks arrived on 7th January, as recommended by HMI on 18th September.

On 14th January three boys passed the entrance examination for the Grammar School.

A boy had left school after passing his labour exam, his parents giving his age as 13, but he was not 13 until the following May so he was ordered by the attendance officer to return to school.

The Fire Brigade gave a demonstration in the Antinghams at 3 o'clock on 7th February. (The Antinghams had a pond at that time.) The boys were let out to see it.

On 9th March the head noted that every boy on the registers had been present since Wednesday afternoon, a minor record. The percentage for the week was 98%.

HM Inspector visited on 19th March and remarked that the light was not particularly good in the upper classroom and suggested that the east window be enlarged. He also suggested a way in which the ventilation of the lower room could be improved. He expressed an opinion that the boys were doing good work and were very intelligent. He was particularly pleased with the mental arithmetic of the upper standard. When his report was received on 8th April, it said that a distinct improvement was evident in the school, but many more desks needed replacing as it was impossible for the boys to work properly on the old equipment. Fireguards were also needed. Ventilators in the lower

Boys of Swaffham National School circa 1908

classroom were recommended. The faults in the premises should be put right at an early date.

The Diocesan Inspector's report in April said the school thoroughly deserved the mark 'Excellent'. All classes were 'excellent'. There were 191 boys on the roll on 19th April. Over 98% attendance had been recorded for the past week.

The boys gave a concert in the Assembly Rooms on 1st and 2nd May. On the second evening medals and prizes were issued by Miss Katherine Knyvet Wilson. The first evening was not very well attended, but the second evening was better. Many items were encored on the second evening.

The first nature walk took place, for standard 2, on 28th May; the next class went on 10th June.

When school resumed in September, some boys were absent working on the late harvest. This continued for two weeks.

1908

On 24th January 168 boys were on the register. There is little of note to repeat. Mr Pheasant was a far better reporter! Even the county inspector's report is not included in the log book.

Rev. Frederick Keeling Scott made his first visit to the school on 20th March.

All departments were closed for three weeks by order of Dr Thomas, owing to measles. There were 45 children absent out of 185 on 15th June. When the school reopened there were still 31 children absent.

The annual Agricultural and Horticultural Show attracted many boys on the afternoon of 16th July.

After the summer holiday, the school reopened early (on 31st August) because of the three-week 'measles' closure, but the harvest was not yet finished as the weather had been bad.

School library books were lent out for the first time on 2nd October.

The HM Inspector report criticised the ventilation. Systematic ventilation, both inlet and outlet, should be improved. The lighting should receive consideration at the same time.

The medical officer of Health sent an order to exclude boys from two groups of cottages on Watton Road, owing to scarlet fever.

The rooms of the school were measured by a County Council inspector on 27th November. (The schoolrooms were measured again by G. Johnson, his purpose not known.)

Herbert Thompson and Frank Savage were absent to attend the distribution of prizes in the Bird and Tree Scheme. The former was a prize-winner.

1909

School reopened on 11th January after an outbreak of scarlet fever in the town during the holidays. On 20th, one of the pupil teachers attended the funeral of Lord Amherst (a noted book collector who had been born at Narford Hall and was to be buried in the family vault at Didlington).

The school sports fund received a grant of ten shillings from the school managers on 12th March.

A note was received from the Education Committee saying, in essence, that any parents who wished to withdraw their children from the Ash Wednesday and Lent services in the church had to do so in writing on each occasion and this is recorded in the register.

On 24th March HM Inspector visited. He condemned the old desks in the classroom, but was told they were being gradually replaced.

On 20th April a new intake of 26 children arrived from the Infants school. There were 176 children present out of 187.

The school again gained the mark 'Excellent' from the Diocesan Inspector on his report received on 28th April.

The Head Teacher met with an accident to his knee, necessitating his absence from school for a few days. His replacement was Mr. A. R. East (Cert. Asst.)

The managers at a meeting on 7th May decided to award a prize to one boy in each class for the best boy in scripture.

Mrs H. Lee Warner awarded prizes for attendance, Vice-Admiral Sir A. K. Wilson being unavoidably absent. Three boys won watches for five years and other prizes were distributed for regular and punctual attendance for four, three, two and one year. The watch winners were Percy Hunn, H. Thompson, and G. Horsley.

The gardening classes were still taking place when possible.

A library book was destroyed on 8th June, having been in a house infected with scarlet fever. Attendance was low on 2nd July as there was a great deal of sickness in the town. Whooping cough appears to have been on the increase.

On 21st July Mr Fenton called to discuss the formation of evening school. On 28th the registers were checked by Miss Katherine Knyvett Wilson.

When school reopened in September, 25 boys were absent because of the late harvest.

Mr Blockley gave ten shillings to the garden boys on behalf of the managers. The first was E. Layern (five shillings), the second was L. Spooner (three shillings) and the third was F. Evans (two shillings).

By 11th September 25–30 boys were still away in the harvest fields; attendance was very poor at 77.3%; two or three cases of whooping cough remained and one family had scarlet fever. Most boys had returned by 1st October.

The HMI's report on drawing was very good, but he said the lighting was very poor in the school in the latter part of the day.

1910

On 8th February Mr Culling, a manager, visited the school and said that a teacher had boxed a boy's ear and then pushed him, so that he fell and knocked his head. The teacher admitted pushing the boy but said that he had previously told him to hasten. He did not intend to push him down, the boy stumbled. The teacher expressed his sorrow and regret, while the head teacher pointed out the serious consequences that might occur.

A Church of England Temperance Society lesson on temperance was given to the school in the afternoon. The effects of alcohol on the mouth and digestion were the subjects of the talk.

During the week ending 23rd March 99% attendance was attained.

Staff list (4th April):
>   Horace Wm. Coe *Certificated (trained) Head Teacher*
>   Arthur Robert East *Certified Assistant*
>   Thomas E. Williamson *Uncertified teacher*
>   Robert H. Limeburn *Uncertified teacher*
>   Mary A. Wright *Uncertified teacher*
>   Arthur C. Davidson *Pupil teacher*

(Davidson was attending the P.T. centre at Hamond's Grammar School from 1st April 1st to 31st December.) Following the staff list is a 'brief outline of the scheme of work, which is shown in detail in a book kept for that purpose'. A list of books follows, covering such subjects as, literature, geography, history, nature study, arithmetic, composition, recitation, singing, physical exercises and drawing.

On 5th April 24 boys were admitted, all but one from the Infants' School.

A parent had complained to a manager that his boy had been punished and marked with a cane. The head teacher explained the nature of the offence and the amount of punishment.

On Ascension Day, a service was held in the Church from 9 to 9.30 a.m. Eighty-five boys, whose parents had given written notice, attended the service.

The Diocesan Inspector visited on 6th May and, as usual, gave a very good report, with a few exceptions. He found the boys quick and intelligent; a list is given in the log book of boys who had distinguished themselves.

An entry on 9th May records: 'His Majesty King Edward 7th died on Friday night last. On Saturday morning, the school flag was hoisted half-mast high. A few words were spoken by the Head Teacher and later that day a telegram was dispatched to Her Majesty, Queen Alexandra at Buckingham Palace. "The Managers, Teachers and Children of the National Schools Swaffham, desire me to express their profound Sympathy with your Majesty in your sad bereavement. Signed 'Head Master.'"' The log book also notes the telegram received in reply.

Mrs H. Lee Warner presented prizes for regular attendance and punctuality. The boys who gained medals for attendance are listed, with Percy Hunn receiving his medal for perfect attendance for six consecutive years.

On 28th June 181 boys were on the roll.

Nature Studies were undertaken by nearly all standards.

On 21st July the boys had a Sunday school treat in the afternoon; the boys were dismissed at 11.35.

Attendance was affected when the Grammar School held their sports and the Primitive Methodists held their school treat.

Mr Green of the Nurseries in Swaffham sent in his award for the best gardens.

The very unsettled weather caused harvest to be finished late, causing about 24 boys to be absent being engaged in harvesting; 32 boys were absent altogether out of a total of 165. About 20 boys were still engaged in harvesting on 23rd September. Several boys had left the neighbourhood. The harvest had finished by 30th September and the boys were back in school.

Mr Vesey visited the school on 3rd October to inspect the physical exercises on behalf of the Board of Education.

Thirteen boys went from school to Lynn to attend the annual Bird and Tree Festival on 2nd December. No teachers accompanied them, as a decision of the managers was not to close the school on account of so few boys.

1911

A boy was struck on the face with a tuning fork on 17th January, puncturing the skin and causing the cheek to swell. The teacher admitted this, but it was not intended as a punishment, merely to call the boy's attention to the lesson. The blow was harder than he intended and he apologised. The Head Teacher pointed out that he must not strike a boy at all.

Whooping cough in two boys caused them to be excluded. The medical officer ruled that only those suffering from whooping cough need be excluded.

About 120 boys attended church at 9 a.m. on 1st March, though the log book gives no explanation.

The report on 10th February from Mr A. E. Kenney Herbert, HMI, included this verdict on the premises:

> 1. The school is on two floors. To reach the upper floor there is but one staircase – a broad wooden one, encased in a wooden building. It would be a death trap if fire were to break out.
>
> Lighting The lighting is inadequate in every room. The gas has to be lighted whenever the day is gloomy. The large room downstairs has a floor area of 1,120 sq. ft., the glass are is not much more than 80 sq. ft., while the room upstairs corresponding in size, has a glass area of about 100 sq. ft. only. Here the gas is often lighted at 10 a.m. in winter.
>
> In the lower room the windows are 6' 4" above the floor. They might well be lowered and some of them enlarged.
>
> It would appear from the temperature records that the warming is inadequate in each of the rooms. The record in the upper large room only shows 10 days and that is January 30th to February 10th. The lowest temperature at 9 a.m. is 40 degrees. This mark was touched twice. Once it has been as high as 49 and once 47. On all other occasions the record is between 40 and 47. At 2 p.m. the recorded temperature has reach 53 once only, and 51 once only.
>
> The desks in the upper room are of a bad type.
>
> Instruction There is evidence of much careful and sound work in this school. Though certain simplifications are advisable

Bookplate from a prize awarded to Percy Naylor, age 8, in 1912. The book was Over the Down *by the prolific Emma Marshall (a Quaker, born at Hill House in Northrepps), first published by Nelson in 1885.*

in the syllabus, especially in science, recitation and history, the scheme of work has been well thought out, and most of the lessons seen were of an intelligent type. It was found that the squared paper in use was inaccurate, which accounted, no doubt, for some poor measuring by the boys in the second class. Much of the drawing deserves praise, but it is suggested that guidelines should no longer be used.

Special praise should be given to the curriculum and timetable for the lowest class. The class teacher is working enthusiastically on the new lines, and the interest and pains she takes in preparing her work is worthy of recognition. The class is doing well under her care. The prospects of the school seem to be very hopeful for the future.

Stamped GNR Dispatched 2nd March 1911.

Attached is the following letter:

Sir, I am directed to forward a copy of a report made by HM Inspector on the above school. Proposals should be submitted as soon as possible for making the upper floor of the boys' department safe in case of fire. I am to enquire what steps will be taken to make the lighting and heating of the boys' department satisfactory.

HM Inspector Kenny Herbert and the managers came to school at 3.40 on 22nd March; the boys were dismissed at 3.45 and an informal meeting was held. New desks (16 at 4' 5") and a cupboard arrived on 10th April.

A selection of drawings, plans of fields etc. was sent to the Education Offices on 30th May with a view to being exhibited in the Royal Agricultural Show.

School closed from 21st June until 3rd July to celebrate the coronation.

Mr East, a certificated assistant since November 1905, terminated his duties to take a position as Head Teacher at St John's School, Lowestoft. A clock and barometer were presented to him.

'Wholesome and hearty amusement' was provided for the boys after school one day by Mr Lee Belmont.

1912

On 8th January there were 169 scholars on roll, 165 present.

The first meeting of the Local Medical Committee was held in the Girls' School on 11th March, to see that the Act for the Improvement in the Health of the Children was more thoroughly carried out.

There are frequent references to the weather and the gardening class; one notable point was that peas were soaked in red lead (to kill insects and pests) before planting.

On a roll of 178, attendance was 96%. It was rare for attendance to drop below 90%, even in the middle of winter; the pupils still had a half-day off for each month of attendance over 90%.

The Diocesan Inspector still examined the children every year and the school always had a good report, sometimes 'excellent'. Standard 1 acted in costume the story of 'The Selling of Joseph'.

In the examinations W. Butters and his older brother, A. Butters, distinguished themselves, as did G. Wilson. (A. Butters wanted to be a parson, but family finances would not allow it.)

The school was closed in the afternoon of 11th July, owing to Sunday school treat. The boys went to Hunstanton. Forty boys were absent on 18th July, going to the local Horticultural Show.

The Salvation Army treat – the first recorded in the log books – took place on 25th July in the afternoon.

On 1st August, a pupil's father claimed that a pupil teacher struck his son. He was assured that the matter would be fully dealt with, and left apparently satisfied. On Thursday evening he took out a summons, which the head teacher endeavoured to get withdrawn. Mr Culling opposed the withdrawal, but later in the day the father withdrew on receiving a written apology and the cost of the summons.

Several boys were absent on 6th August, four or five owing to the harvest. The weather became so wet that harvest was still not finished on 16th September and 26 boys were away on that morning.

A reference was made to the ringing of the school bell; the first was rung at 8.45 and the second at 8.56. The afternoon bells were rung at 1.40 and 1.47 p.m.

From 29th November the gardening class was suspended for a time, except for occasional lessons.

1913

On 14th January the head complained that Leonard Brightwell was late again in the afternoon. He worked in the dinner hour, running errands for Mr Philo, then went home for dinner before returning to school.

Mr Philo said the boy went home for dinner at 1 o'clock and there was no excuse for being late.

There are many entries regarding the timing of the ringing of the bell. On 7th February, the first bell was not rung – Mr Weddall was responsible.

On 1st April 26 children came from the Infants School, but the head teacher complained that several of them did not know their letters and only about half had a fair idea about numbers.

The new curriculum included English, arithmetic, singing, physical exercises and geography in all classes, together with nature study in standards 1 to 4 and history in standards 2 to 7. Gardening was also taken practically by 14 boys. Drawing as a subject had been dropped, but was taught in connection with other lessons where needed. Nature study as a subject for the upper standards had been dropped, as had history for the lower standards.

On 2nd May the attendance was only 82%, and shortly thereafter a telegram and letter from the school Medical Officer closed the school because of the measles outbreak. This closure lasted from 5th to 19th May; when the school reopened, there were still 20 boys absent out of 175 on the register. During the holiday the school had been thoroughly cleaned and sprinkled with Jeyes Fluid. However, on 30th May Reg Drake had to be excluded for measles. The attendance was reduced to 88.4%.

On 30th June 93 prizes were awarded, all the schools attending on the Vicarage lawn. The vicar distributed the prizes.

The Salvation Army laid on a treat on 11th July, resulting in ten boys being absent.

Swaffham Flower Show on 24th July meant a half-holiday for the boys, many of whom exhibited bunches of wild flowers.

A box of vegetables and specimens of notebooks and weather charts were sent to Norwich by train for exhibition.

Rev. D. M. Heath offered five shillings towards a set of wickets for the boys.

School closed for the harvest holidays on 8th August – the harvest had started, and attendance had dropped to 89%.

The formation of a woodwork centre was discussed at a meeting in September, and on 1st October a class of 20 boys began woodwork classes in the Shirehall under Mr W. Baker.

Only 84 children were at school in the afternoon when 'Lord' John Sanger's circus visited the town.

The school bell was broken.

On 14th November, Nurse Bullock examined the heads of all the children, returning on 10th December to examine 'special children'.

Bostock & Wombwell's menagerie were back again on their regular visit. A half-holiday was given because of this.

1914

In January the Head Teacher was stopped by Mr J. Ripper, who discussed his son's health. (This would be Ben Ripper, author of *Ribbons from the Pedlar's Pack* (Downham Market: Quaker Press, 1972).)

On 28th January in the afternoon, standard 1 visited the Market Place for a lesson.

The HMI report of February referred to many buildings that presented difficulties, but the boys' work was satisfactory, the head teacher set a high standard and the assistants worked hard.

Mr and Mrs Pheasant came to present the prizes at the annual prizegiving on the vicarage lawn.

By the end of September builders making alterations in the school were a fortnight behind as it was difficult obtaining materials due to the railways being required for the movement of troops etc. One of the teachers was away serving in the RAMC.

1915

On 7th January one of the teachers, W. B. Clarke, is recorded as enlisting in His Majesty's forces.

On 27th January the police (acting under military instructions) said there must be no bright lights in the schools after 5 o'clock. Consequently, the afternoon session was begun earlier and slight alterations were made to the timetable.

Mr Edgar A. Coe (brother of the head teacher), a certified assistant, began work in the school on 17th February but finished on 5th March.

A. Spinks, while being punished, struggled and knocked his face between the eyes on a desk.

A new set of registers was started on 1st April with 154 pupils on the roll. This increased to 179 after the Easter holidays. At the first morning session after Easter 170 were present.

On Ascension Day the children were somewhat later from church. (The children's attendance at church reduced considerably, but there were still occasions when they attended. On this day only 30 children were in school at 9 o'clock.)

A delivery from Jarrolds on 17th May contained 3 quires (1,480 sheets per quire) of paper and half a gross (72) of exercise books – the days of the slate were over.

An entry on 18th June noted that a soldiers' camp had been laid out on the Antinghams.

The Royal Norfolk Show was held in Fakenham on 22nd and 23rd June. A box of six sorts of vegetables from the school gardens were sent, plus a boy's notebook of his gardening work, a plan of the school gardens and a plan of an individual plot.

The Band of the Sherwood Rangers, by kind permission of Col. Dawson, played selections at the annual prize giving at the Vicarage Lawn. They had assembled outside the Boys' School at 2.45 and headed a procession, via the Shirehall, to the Vicarage. The boys marched four abreast, the girls and infants falling in at the corner of the Shirehall Green. The boys and the girls contributed national songs of the Allies and the infants, some interesting and amusing games. This was the last time prizes were to be awarded for good attendance by the Norfolk Education Committee, which now believed that prizes should be given for merit and industry and should be awarded by the head teachers. It was reported that only £11 out of the total of £394 had still to be found for the alterations to the Boys' School. Some 52 boys received prizes from Mrs Murray Gawme, one of the managers, who commissioned the head teacher to purchase a Union Jack.

One of the teachers, R. H. Limeburn, had to report to Britannia Barracks, Norwich for examination. However he was back at school the next day having been rejected by the military doctor because of his eyesight.

On 12th July Miss Nora Layern, who had just completed training at Norwich, began work at the school. Previous teachers had all been male, but the war caused a shortage of men.

On 29th October, owing to regulations regarding lighting on account of the war, the morning session (from 29th October) closed at 11.45, the last lesson being curtailed. The afternoon session finished at 3.15 instead of 5 o'clock.

On 7th December the boy's football was accidentally kicked onto the roof of the passage between the school and Mrs Offord's house; in the afternoon playtime, Fred Youngs was found cutting the wire netting that prevented the ball from being retrieved. He was punished.

The attendance for the quarter ending 31st December 1915 was 93.8%.

1916

Mr Limeburn went away on active service on 29th February.

On 17th March there was much sickness, with 18 boys absent the whole week. The attendance was the lowest this year at 82.3%. By the end of the month the head teacher was recording the lowest weekly percentage since 27th June 27th, due to several cases of sickness and measles, as well as the worst blizzard in living memory. Considerable damage was done by the northerly wind and many trees were blown down.

Details from reports 1916–55

The log books from 1916 to 1950 are missing, but some details have survived in various school reports.

1927

October 24th **The staff of this school has changed considerably since the last report was written. At the present time the Head Master** [John Harker] **is assisted by an efficient staff** [with two senior classes downstairs and the younger boys upstairs in two and, later, three classes]. **The provision of home-made maps for the geography lessons and illustrations for the teaching of history deserves commendation.** [The Inspector (R. S. Reade) is generally favourable in his comments, reporting that a lot of lost ground due to various illnesses has been caught up by the senior boys.]

1929

[The Headmaster is praised for the improvement in the scholars, despite the overcrowding.] **The loyal and earnest efforts of the assistant teachers, the readiness displayed to move with the times and ensure consideration for the needs of all the scholars are having very fruitful results.**

The improved supply of books for History and Geography, and the provision of excellent illustrations, deserve mention.

[There is a lot of repetition in the reports, especially concerning the overcrowding.]

1930

In spite of the difficulties peculiar to this school and the staffing dislocation due to the absence of one or more assistant teachers, a reasonable standard of attainment can be recorded in all classes.

1934

There is no change in the working conditions of this school. The senior boys are taught in a large, undivided room on the ground floor, two classes are also accommodated in the room above, and an intermediate division occupies a badly lighted space walled off from the classes upstairs. The open space from which access to the school is gained, serves as a playground, but this is open to the public and its usefulness is marred by the uneven nature of the surface.

[The Boys' School, Campingland, closed on 6th April 1955 when all Senior boys were transferred to Swaffham Secondary Modern School.]

Infants' School 1873–1936

1873

Head teacher – Miss Trotter.

19th September   School commenced on Monday morning with an attendance of 47, which increased as the week advanced. Three girls taken on trial for a month as monitors with a view to becoming Pupil Teachers.

November 7th   School closed on Wednesday because of cattle fair and on Thursday afternoon because of a circus, to which the children were partly treated; attendance rather poor rest of week.

1874

March 13th Snow all week and attendance very low in consequence.

20th School as usual until Friday afternoon when children had a holiday given them, because of a circus visiting the town.

April 10th School closed Easter Monday afternoon – and school as usual rest of week.

May 1st Several children sick with a kind of fever – two belonging to the IV class died with it – William Oxborough and Florence Thurgood.

15th Summary of Inspector's Report: 'This very promising school supplies what has hitherto been much wanted for the education of the poor in this parish. Miss Trotter has begun her work in it, in a very satisfactory manner.'

July 24th School as usual, except on Thursday afternoon when it was closed on account of a tea in connection with Labourers' Union, most of children going.

1875

January 8th School began with thin attendance due to Whooping cough.

29th Neither class nearly full, but fair progress made this week. Class III began to read in books.

May 14th No school on Wednesday on account of cattle fair.

28th Summary of Inspector's Report: 'This is a good school in which the children are well looked after and well taught.'

June 18th Nothing unusual occurred this week, except that the children were prevented from going into the playground each day because of the grass being wet.

October 29th Second class began writing in copybooks.

1876

January 25th I, M. A. Smythe, commenced my work as mistress of the Swaffham Infants' School.

March 17th E. A. Anderson commenced work as mistress of Swaffham Infants' School.

May 15th Miss Clark took charge today. Average number of children 108.

June 12th Wednesday and Thursday gave holiday on account of the Agricultural Show being held in the town.

June 19th School as usual on Monday. Attendance very good at 118, several children admitted and two returned after a long absence.

The following is the report made by Mr Hill (Inspector), after his visit April 1876: The frequent change of mistresses has somewhat weakened this school, but it is still in good order, and on the whole, well taught.

School staff: Miss Clark *Certificated Mistress*
                  L. Thurgood *Pupil Teacher end of second year*
                  E. Dickerson *PT end of second year*
                  E. Wharton *PT end of first year*

June 23rd Average lowered considerably owing to the heavy rain.

July 3rd Admitted several children. Children sent to see some soldiers who came into the town Wednesday and Friday.

July 10th Children sent on Monday to see the band of the Carabineers.

1877

January 11th School opened on Monday by Pupil Teachers after two weeks holiday. Mistress unable to return until Tuesday owing to illness in her family.

February 5th Ten children have been admitted since January, plus several children returned to school after several weeks' absence.

19th Attendance very bad throughout week, owing to extremely rough weather.

March 19th Pupil teachers examination on Saturday 24th at quarter to four to allow teachers to go away, as they were going to Lynn overnight.

April 2nd Half-holiday on Monday being bank holiday, also on Thursday owing to the opening of new organ (in Church).

April 23rd Seven children admitted (This means 33 children admitted since Easter)

School inspected by HMI Mr. F. Myers, attendance 143.

[Children constantly being admitted and others being re-admitted. Others, being of the right age, were transferred to the upper schools.]

June 18th The summary of the report received after HM Inspector's visit is as follows:- This school is well taught and disciplined. The arithmetic of the first class deserves special praise.

Average attendance 140.

1878

April 12th Resigned my situation as Mistress of Swaffham Infants' School, Elizabeth H. Clark.

15th Selina H. Brian commenced duty as teacher of the Swaffham Infants School.

July 1st I, Eliza Cook, commenced teaching in Swaffham Infants School - number of children present 109.

HM Inspector report: 'School continues to be very well taught and disciplined. The reading and arithmetic of the first and second classes deserve praise. The writing should be larger and rounder.'

October 17th Today I relinquish charge of Swaffham Infants' School. Signed Eliza Cook.

21st I, Elizabeth Ann Pain, took charge of Swaffham Infants' School this 21st day of October.

1879

January 6th Reopened school after a fortnight's holiday, received payment from Miss Day and Miss Wilson for children in the school.

[HMI report in April:] 'The Infants are in very good order and they appear to be well taught. The first and second classes are well advanced. There is, however, a weakness in having so many children of six years old in the second and third classes. It should be quite an exception for a child of six years to be in the first class.'

July 14th Only 56 children present, owing to the Baptist Sunday school treat.

21st Very wet. Only 30 children present.

Small school all the week owing to the unfavourable weather, and the prevailing disease of measles among the children. Average attendance for the week 57.8. [Note – school not closed down because of measles, as it would be later.]

August 11th School still badly attended owing to the measles. Average attendance for the week 38.

August 22nd Harvest Holiday. I resign charge of Swaffham Infants School this day, Elizabeth A. Pain.

September 29th Alice Payne commenced duties as Temporary Mistress of this school.

October 6th Miss Wilson visited the school and paid school place for four children.

13th – 17th Attendance improving – several children returned to school, having been absent some weeks; several admissions. Punished several children in first class for copying arithmetic.

November 3rd – 7th A boy admitted, Miss Montagu promising to pay half his school money i.e. 1d per week.

December 18th School closed on Thursday afternoon for the Christmas holidays. Accounts all made up and cashbook sent to the Rector.

 I resign my charge of the Swaffham Infants School this day December 18th 1879; A. S. Payne.

1880

I, Knighton Curtis, commenced my duties as mistress of Swaffham Infants School January 5th 1880. [This mistress followed the example set by her predecessor in that she only made entries in the logbook once a week, on Friday.]

19th – 23rd January Attendance very poor throughout the week. Average only 66.6. [So it continued until . . .]

February 9th – 13th Attendance better throughout the week. Children went out to play on Wednesday and Friday.

March 15 – 19th Average attendance for the week 110.

April 7th Her Majesty's Inspector examined the school in the morning and gave the children a holiday in the afternoon. Rev. G. R. Winter visited in the morning. The attendance was 120. [The Vicar, or his wife and/or daughter, were regular visitors.]

May 10 – 14th Not a good school this week. A holiday was given on Wednesday being Cattle Fair Day.

24 –28th H.M. Inspector's report received on May 29th: -

Infants' School – The Infants' school is in a seriously worse condition than it has been for the last two years. This may be accounted for by the frequent change of Teachers and by the circumstance to which I called attention at the end of my last report. I shall expect all the classes to be much more forward next year. Sewing is very poor.

School staff: **Knighton Curtis** *Certificated*
                 Ellen Wharton *P.T. end of 5th year.*
                 Elizabeth M. More *P.T. end of 1st year.*
                 Emily Spencer *Candidate.*
         The latter passed the examination for admission as Pupil Teacher.
         Ellen Wharton is now qualified under Article 79.

September 20th School opened after the harvest holidays. [Late this year probably because of the late harvest.]

September 27 to October 1st Holiday on Thursday afternoon being Harvest Thanksgiving Day.

October 11th – 15th Three ladies sent in school fees for the same number of children for past quarter.

1881

Jan 31st – February 4th Some new books and slates bought.

March 28th – April 1st Miss G. Montagu and some friends visited on Monday afternoon.

May 9th – 13th [Summary of Inspector's Report received on May 18th 1881:] 'The school has made progress on the whole, but there is still room for improvement. The reading both in the First and Second Classes is poor, and the discipline might be a little firmer.'

July 11th The Rev. Gwynne came in after the children were dismissed.

August 1 – 5th Closed school on Friday afternoon for Harvest Holiday.

I resign charge of Swaffham Infants' School on the same day. Signed K. Curtis.

September 12th Commenced duties in this school with an attendance of 105 and 106 respectively. M. E. Page.

September 19th No recreation in the playground on account of disorder.

October 4th Dismissed school at 11 o'clock, for the rest of the day, a holiday being given in consequence of the marriage of the vicar's daughter.

November 23rd Punished C. Nelson and C. Butters for loitering on the road in coming to school and thus causing themselves to be late.

December 1st several children kept in for disobedience.

1882

13th January 10 names withdrawn from registers, on account of the children's continued absence.

30th Good attendance. Notice given by the Land Surveyor, that none of the children living in Bull Yard (behind 'Horse and Groom') are to attend school, fever being among the inhabitants.

6th February Good attendance, notwithstanding the compulsory absence of the Nelsons, Burroughs, and Lushers through Scarlet Fever.

27th School gradually increases in number.

April 3rd G. Dickerson and A. Crafer were absent through illness.

17th Two of the managers called with an order from the doctor to close the school tonight, on account of the prevalence of scarlet fever in the town, until further notice.

May 22nd School reopened, by the sanction of the medical men with the restriction that no child is allowed to attend school for a month from this date, who has recently suffered from fever or has had fever in the house.

30th Holiday given in the afternoon, by reason of the Foresters' Club demonstration.

June 19th A child's father has conformed to the rule of the school and paid the fine of 1/1d. because his child was absent on the day of examination without leave.

July 3rd Numbers much reduced by the many cases of indisposition among the little ones, some are suffering from colds and others, scarletina.

19th Holiday all day, being the Cattle Fair.

27th Number on registers 193 (showing a gradual increase overall).

29th September Number on registers 214.

6th October All the children living in Bull Yard absent from school today, owing to another case of fever among the residents.

23rd Reproved the pupil teachers for repeating their home lessons imperfectly.

November 2nd Punished two children for pilfering and telling falsehoods.

6th A boy of 8 years of age returned to school today having been absent since July 14th. He scarcely knows his letters. Taken 24 names off the registers on account of continued absence.

10th The brother of the above boy has returned to school, has been absent the same length of time as his brother.

4th December Six children have returned to school, after some months' absence. All of them are 7 years of age and scarcely know a letter. Attendance Officer called to inquire if certain children were present.

18th Although there are many absentees, yet the attendance is unusually good for the last week before the holidays. Sent an 'Enquiry Sheet' to everyone absent from school.

20th Issued the 'Rules of the School' to every child present this morning.

1883

January 9th Admitted A. Moulton. Punished three truant boys.

15th Admitted C. Perkins. Sent an enquiry sheet to all the children who absented themselves on account of the rain.

22nd Mistress leaving at 12-o'clock to attend a meeting of the Attendance Committee held at the Union.

31st The progress of the class is much retarded by the backward children who have been admitted during the year from the Private Schools at the age of 7 years, when they must be presented in Standard I.

March 9th Number on registers 179. The names of 33 children sent to the Attendance Officer for irregular attendance. [This became a weekly part of the Head Teacher's tasks. Truancy was far more vigorously dealt with than before.]

April 6th Seven names of irregular children sent to the Clerk to the Board of Guardians. (No attendance officer at present.)

9th Attendance larger this week than it has ever been.

13th Average attendance 160.3, number on registers 186. Of this number, only ten children have been absent all the week. Their names sent to the new Attendance Officer.

16th Good attendance. Absentees sent after.

25th Children sent out to play for a quarter of an hour. [An unusual reference. Did children have 'playtime' previously?] Several cases of sickness reported.

May 3rd Visited by the Attendance Officer, who paid the fees of the non-pauper children.

28th Thirteen cases of measles have been reported and twelve children are absent through the fever or measles being in the family.

29th First lesson in geography given by E. Moore to the first class.

June 21st Only 116 children were present in the morning. Visited by the Attendance Officer, who gave out to the children, that rain was no excuse for absenting themselves. [Absenteeism during rain was often due to inadequate clothing and boots or shoes as well as the state of the roads, which were reduced to muddy tracks impassable for small children.]

22nd Visited again by the Attendance Officer, average attendance 141.2, number on registers 186.

July 3rd Commenced a course of natural history and object lessons.

9th Absentees sent after. Nine children absent through sore heads and ringworm.

10th Commenced Kindergarten games in recreation time.

19th Holiday given in the afternoon, by reason of the Choral Festival held in the Church.

20th Forty-four names of irregular children sent to the attendance officer this week. [Possibly start of harvest?]

August 2nd Commenced school at 1.30pm today instead of 2-o'clock, to afford the teachers and children an opportunity of attending the bazaar held in the Vicarage Grounds.

17th October **Miss G. Montagu visited the school.** [Miss Montagu was becoming a regular and stalwart supporter of the school, even teaching sewing.]

18th E. Moore (A) attempted to give a Natural History lesson to the upper section of the school, but the children were so disorderly the lesson had to be discontinued and given after school hours.

29th Only 71 present in the afternoon, owing to Ginnett's Circus being in the town.

November 1st Names of six children withdrawn from registers on account of continued absence and death.

6th A child was admitted from the Union [workhouse].

December 14th Fred Diaper's name withdrawn from register, having died suddenly after a few hours illness. Five children have died within the last two months and many are still absent through sickness.

1884

January 18th A child was excused from the reading lessons, on account of defective eyesight, caused by a recent illness.

23rd Both sections of standard I wrote in copybooks at the same time this morning, the new desks fixed yesterday affording accommodation for that purpose.

February 8th Gave Geography lesson to standard I on the 'Boundaries of the School room'. [One of the first geography lessons.]

11th Attendance much better. Only six children absent themselves now on account of delicacy of health after an illness, the others have returned.

March 14th Several children absented themselves this afternoon to gather violets.

April 10th Broke up in the afternoon till the 15th (Tuesday) for the Easter Holidays. [First mention of a holiday at this time. Previously only a half-day was given.]

18th Gave the first lesson in 'Language'.

28th The Attendance Officer brought a list of children of five years and upwards, to whose parents he had issued notices, in order to enforce their attendance at school.

30th Miss Turnour visited the school to hear the children sing. [First time.]

7th May 'The Infants school is in a satisfactory condition on the whole. The second division of the first standard is backward. A good deal is done to vary and brighten the occupations of the children. Chiefly on this account I recommend a Good Merit Grant.'

12th Lowest class in the school allowed recreation in the playground for a quarter of an hour, this morning.

14th Holiday all day on account of Lamb Fair.

22nd May Children allowed recreation in the playground. No registers marked in the afternoon, owing to the small number of children, occasioned by the demonstration in the town, on the arrival of Captain Wilson, who had just won the Victoria Cross.

June 20th Commenced the Tonic Solfa system.

July 28th Attendance Officer brought the form, giving notice of the period appointed by the attendance committee, in which the Education Act is suspended.

24th October Punished two children for running out of school, when kept in by the teacher.

31st Punished four children for coming late, by keeping them in after school.

December 1st **Owing to a deep snow, only 30 were present this morning. Number on register – 167.**

1885

January 8th **At the close of the school, a bun and an orange were distributed to each child, to celebrate the coming of age of Prince Albert Victor, after an address from the vicar.**

12th **Only 25 children assembled this morning, owing to a heavy fall of snow. Dismissed at 9.45 a.m. for the rest of the day.**

13th **Ten children presented themselves this morning. School closed again. Opened in the afternoon and registers marked.**

16th **Thirty-eight is the number of children present at all during the week, occasioned by a deep snow. List of ninety-seven names sent to the attendance officer. Average attendance 31.4, number on the registers 160.**

February 25th **Corrected several children for loitering on their way to school.**

27th **Urged a Monitoress to greater diligence in teaching her class.**

March 4th **Examined the 2nd Class in 'Reading'.** [Examinations were frequent – the Head Teacher also conducting exams in 'Writing' and 'Number', as well as the assistants examining the children on 'Cardinal Points', 'Course of Natural History' and other subjects learnt throughout the year.]

20th **Two children punished for playing truant.**

April 23rd **Children allowed recreation in the playground.** [At this time the playground was of bare earth or grass, so had to be dry before children could use it.]

May 14th **Summary of Inspector's report: 'The condition of the Infants School is quite satisfactory though some of the children in the second division of the first class are backward. There would appear to be a want of organisation when so many children over seven years of age, and some over eight are found in the lower classes. But it appears that many of them are old when they first come to this school, having previously attended Dame Schools.'**

June 30th **Lessons given on a 'Clock Face' in order to teach children the time of day.**

September 21st **Another child over seven years of age, with no knowledge of the alphabet, came from one of the Dame Schools, but as there was a doubt about the age, she was sent home till the accuracy of it could be proved.**

September 28th **Admitted a girl of 7.5 years, from one of the Dame Schools, and placed her for instruction in the Babies class, as she is ignorant of the alphabet.**

October 7th **Small attendance in the afternoon, owing to the Clothing Club teas given by several tradesmen of the town.**

November 11th **Smaller number in the afternoon, owing to a collection of wild beasts being in the town.**

December 3rd **Holiday given tomorrow, being the Polling Day in Swaffham for the General Election.**

1886

January 11th **Ninety-one has been the highest number of children present at one opening of the school during the week, owing to the severe weather. A child, age 8 years & 7 months, came to school from the Union** [workhouse] **this week ignorant of the alphabet.**

22nd **Continued the instruction of the second division of Standard I. Second and third classes kept in, for undue noise during lessons.**

Average attendance – 130. Number on the registers – 169. Thirty-six names sent to the Attendance Officer.

February 15th **Admitted H. Banner.** [It has become a common occurrence to put in the names of children admitted.] **That brought the total attendance for the day to 145.**

19th **Sixteen cases of Mumps in the school.** [Mumps reduced the attendance for some time.]

March 22nd **Sickness has almost disappeared among the children, only a few cases of Mumps still remain.**

31st **End of school year.**

April 1st **Commenced the new registers. Two or three new cases of mumps.**

12th Drafted thirty-four boys and twenty girls to the Boys' and Girls' Schools. School reorganised.

May 7th School gradually increasing. 'Drawing an animal' again taken this week among the varied occupations.

May 3rd [Summary of the Diocesan Inspector's report:] 'The infants are in good order, and they are taught with very praiseworthy care. The second divisions in both the First and Second classes are backward. The First divisions are well advanced. Sewing deserves a special mention. George R. Winter'

School staff: Martha Ellen Page   *Certified Teacher 1st Class*
                  Emily Spencer *Assistant under Article 50*
                  Pricilla Chatton   ”   ”   ”   84
                  Gertrude Jarvis   *Pupil Teacher 2nd year*
                  Emily Smith   ”   ”   *1st year*

May 12th Holiday all day – Cattle Fair.

13th Wet day. An attendance of 52 and 82 respectively. 'Writing' lesson given in the afternoon from 3.30 p.m. until 4 p.m., instead of the ordinary lesson.

28th Numbers have fluctuated this week, owing to the rainy weather. Average attendance 126.4, on the registers – 158.

June 11th Numbers have been reduced the latter part of the week through the appearance of ringworm among the children.

24th Only 95 children present in the afternoon, owing to the Baptist Sunday school annual treat.

25th Received the quarterly fees of the Pauper children. [From the Union Workhouse and those children whose parents received 'out-relief'. This includes the residents of the several almshouses.]

July 13th Several cases of measles reported.

28th Registers marked at 9.15 a.m. instead of 9.45 a.m. to allow for the dismissal of the school at 11.30 a.m., on the occasion of the Sunday school treat.

30th Attendance further reduced this week by the increase of measles. 42 children absent.

August 1st **Bank Holiday**

5th Attendance poor, owing to the commencement of Harvest.

October 4th Good attendance of one hundred and fifty two children.

5th Several children punished for being late back to school in the afternoon.

22nd Examined the 1st division of 7 year old children in 'Dictation'. Kept in several children of the 7-year-old children for 'Spelling'.

29th Discontinued the instruction of the PTs from 7 a.m. to 8 a.m.

November 8th Commenced the instruction of the PTs at 4.30 p.m.

12th Punished five children for coming to school after the Registers were closed.

15th No child has come too late for registration.

December 3rd Usual number of children attended the first part of the week, but owing to the severity of the weather; the numbers have fallen the last two days.

8th Only 35 children present this morning, by reason of a heavy downpour of rain.

1887

January School reopened with a poor attendance occasioned by the snow and frost.

24th I. Chatton, teacher under Art[icle] 84, left the school, owing to domestic circumstances. Vacancy supplied by a mistress on trial. [Several teachers came and went. This is just one of them.]

February 25th 'Drawing' lesson again given to upper section of the school instead of the second Object Lesson.

April 12th School reopened after Easter holidays. 33 boys and 28 girls sent up to the Boys' and Girls' School. Not received by the Master & Mistress. School reorganised.

13th Children drafted at 10.00 a.m. this morning by order of the Master.

Two children sent back from the other schools.

25th School slowly fills up again. 18 children have been admitted since the draft of 61 to the other schools.

27th Summary of Inspector's Report: 'Infants' School: The Infants continue to do well, on the whole though, as usual, there is a considerable number of backward children in the second division of the first two classes. This appears to result from the late age at which many are sent to school.'

June 24th Attendance much smaller this week, occasioned by the Jubilee Celebrations in Swaffham & the neighbourhood.

July 21st Only 105 in attendance in the afternoon, owing to the Wesleyan Sunday school Treat [just 4 more than the previous week, 14th, when the Baptist Sunday school treat was held].

August 4th Holiday in the afternoon, on account of the Sunday school Treat. [This would have been the Church of England Sunday school treat. Note that in the previous two weeks the non-conformist churches' treats did not warrant a holiday, just a reference to absenteeism because of them.]

September 15th Gave the first lesson in the Tonic Solfa system to the 1st & 2nd classes.

October 7th 'Drawing' taken in Standard I from 3.30 to 4 p.m. instead of the ordinary lesson specified on timetable.

28th Out of one hundred and seventy six on the books, only one hundred and forty one have been present at all, owing to sickness among the children and the rainy weather.

November 11th Out of 169 names of children on the Registers, only 129 have been marked present at all. Of the number of absentees, thirty-five have been reported sick. Whooping cough is still very prevalent and is increasing.

18th Commenced Drawing with rulers in the 1st and 2nd classes.

25th Out of 171 on the Books, only 128 children have been present at all, owing [to] whooping cough etc.

December 2nd Practised the Christmas Carols.

1888

January 9th Only a few cases of whooping cough remain.

20th Geography lessons have been discontinued in the upper division of the school, and Solfa lessons have been given instead.

February 10th Tuning fork used for the first time in the Tonic Solfa lessons.

24th Two names withdrawn from Register, the children having left the Union.

March 5th Attendance Officer called in answer to a note requesting him to send to school all the children who had absented themselves several weeks on account of the severe weather. One child returned to school after four months absence.

16th Divided the 5-year-old children into two sections rendered necessary by the irregularity of many of them during the winter.

19th One child returned to school after seven months absence.

29th End of school year, number on registers – 165.

April 23rd **Two children left for America.** [Emigration to American, Australia and even the industrial Midlands was not uncommon in times of hardship.]

[Between *27th* and *30th*, the mistress wrote in the book a list of songs the children were learning. These included 'I Love My Good and Gracious Queen'.]

30th **Summary of H.M. Inspector's report: 'The Infants continue to be taught with the most praiseworthy care. Singing is very good, also sewing.'**

School Staff: **Martha Ellen Page** *Certified teacher 1st class*
                  Emily Spencer *Assistant under Article 50*
                  Gertrude Jarvis *Pupil Teacher 4th year*
                  Emily Smith *Pupil Teacher 3rd year*
                  Maud Heyhoe *Candidate on Probation*

18th Dismissed school till 28th (Whitsun Holidays).

31st May **Staff at the school to be reduced. Emily Spencer obliged to resign her assistantship in this school.** Number on the registers 156.

July 10th O. Rallison's name withdrawn from register, the family having emigrated to America.

27th Notice placed up the school, to show the period in which children are exempt from the Byelaws.

31st Rev. J. Powell brought the fees paid by the War Office.

17th August Rev. J. Powell present during the marking of registers thus testing the accuracy of them. He then examined the registers and found them correct.

1st October The increase in attendance since the holidays has necessitated the removal of forward children to higher classes. Number on registers 184.

5th December Only 136 children present in the afternoon, occasioned by arrival of Prince George, on a visit to Didlington Hall.

10th One admission. E. Spencer (A) absent in the morning with leave.

1889

April 1st Beginning of school year. Commenced a register of Pupil Teachers instruction, recording time and attendance. A list of lessons approved by H.M. Inspector included.

April 8th Holiday given in the afternoon. (Confirmation, by the Lord Bishop of Norwich.)

10th May Number on registers – 150.

13th Three admissions. School gradually filling up.

20th Four admissions. Attendance good, notwithstanding two or three cases of measles & scarletina have cropped up.

June 7th Registration cancelled in the morning, school being dismissed at 10.45, owing to tempestuous weather.

17th School reopened (after Whitsun holidays) with poor attendance occasioned by preparation for Agricultural Show.

19th Only eighty children present in the morning. Holiday in the afternoon, an Agricultural Show being held in the town.

20th Only fifty-six children present in the morning. Holiday in the afternoon for the same reason as yesterday.

21st Attendance continues poor. The average is only 99.

24th Good attendance.

25th July Only one hundred and twelve in attendance this afternoon, occasioned by the Wesleyan Sunday school treat and the Primrose League Entertainment.

August 2nd G. Jarvis (A) left the school today, for another appointment in Yorkshire.

6th Small attendance, the byelaws with regard to the attendance being in force this week.

Sept 20th One hundred & fifty eight has been the highest number present this week. Reproved a Pupil Teacher for lessons imperfectly done.

27th Number on registers, one hundred and eighty three, but only ninety-one were present in the afternoon, owing to a circus being in the town.

November 4th admitted two Union [workhouse] children. Copy of Byelaws placed up in the school-room.

29th On Wednesday (27th) the attendance was only 15 and 15 respectively, owing to a deep snow. On the last few days the numbers have been better, but still far below the attendance of the first two days of the week.

Average attendance – 99, number on registers –190.

December 20th Attendance remarkably small all week. Broke up until Jan. 6th 1890 for Christmas holidays.

1890

January 24th Attendance less than [last?] week, owing to the prevailing epidemic. Mistress unable to attend school, owing to indisposition.

31st Attendance a trifle better than last week, but still poor, owing to the influenza epidemic [usually referred to as the 'prevailing epidemic'].

February 7th Miss K. Wilson supplied a teaching place Monday afternoon.

17th Number of absentees through sickness on the increase. Four upper classes instructed by Mistress, Assistant and Pupil Teacher this week.

April 18th Number on the registers – 191, average attendance – 155.1.

25th Fifty-eight children drafted to the Boys' and Girls' Schools; School reorganised.

May 2nd Fourteen of the first division commenced to write in copy-books.

12th School gradually re-filling after the draft to upper schools.

16th Summary of Inspector's Report: 'In both the first and second classes there are large second divisions of children who re much behind those of the first. This appears to arise from a number of children being admitted late and backward. Every effort should be made to induce parents to send their children at four years of age at the latest. Otherwise the School is doing well. Reading, however, is slow and inaccurate. Sewing is good.'

June 6th Two divisions made in lowest class of the school on account of its size.

November 28th Attendance low all week, especially so today, the numbers being 40 and 42 respectively, occasioned by a deep snow.

No names sent to the Attendance Officer, because there were 109 names to enter on the returns, owing to sickness and snowy weather.

1891

January 5th School reopened, but owing to the severity of the weather, a very small attendance.

The bad weather continued until the 30th when a favourable change in the weather occurred, but attendance is far below the number expected.

February 2nd Mistress sent in her resignation to the vicar.

6th Letter of thanks received from the Committee, through Mr. A. Winter.

March 6th Three re-admissions and five admissions. These children had been attending one of the Dame Schools in the town, but is now shut.

April 17th Mistress [M. E. Page] resigned the charge of this school today.

May 4th **I, Miriam Jane Spires, commenced my duties as mistress of this school this day.**

[This mistress wrote her notes at the end of the week, whereas her predecessors wrote daily.]

November 20th **Number now on registers 225.**

1892

January 11th School reopened today, owing to the presence of snow. Attendance small.

23rd Attendance has improved considerably this week, considering the state of the weather, the roads too being very slippery and dangerous to little ones.

30th Attendance improved very much this week. The numbers on the books are now – Boys – 119; Girls – 109, total 228.

26th An unusually good attendance this week. On Wednesday afternoon 208 children were present.

April 9th This week has been the highest attendance yet recorded. On Wednesday 210 children were present.

11th One child admitted who had great shyness and very delicate health and having been only to a private school, is as yet nervous among so many children.

27th Number present this morning 222, school closed for remainder of week, on account of Bazaar, at which Standard I will drill and sing.

Object Lessons for 1893 (Groups only): Common Objects, Natural History, Natural Productions, Natural Phenomena, Miscellaneous, Form and Colour, Food and Clothing.

May 11th Holiday given all day, being Swaffham May Fair.

26th Summary of Inspector's report, received on the 25th: 'Infants' School – The classes are crowded and the children are in consequence noisy and inattentive. Maud Heyhoe entirely failed to keep order while giving her lesson. Under more favourable circumstances Miss Spiers will I believe, prove herself to be a good disciplinarian.'

July 9th Owing to the closure of the Boys' & Girls' Schools, the attendances during the latter part of the week have decreased.

15th Many absent on Wednesday the number present was considerably less, this being Election Day. Number on books – 229.

29th Attendance very good, highest number present – 198.

August 12th Attendance lower than usual yesterday owing to 'Auction of Bazaar Remains' and a circus.

October 1st Attendance (till Thursday) numbered either 200 or more. Order of III Class has slightly improved; have received new slates for same class.

22nd One boy re-admitted from Boys' School because of dullness.

29th The whole school examined by me on Friday (with exception of Babies). Notable entry: II Class – Order – Much improved, but still several children fond of talking and looking about, especially during individual reading.

November 6th The Gallery in the classroom has been moved, so as to face the fire place and receive light from right and left, instead of from front and back of children. A new cupboard provided for large room, and locks placed on cupboards in classroom.

December 2nd The attendances were lower than usual on Thursday, owing to heavy rain, but still not poor considering the distance some little ones have to come.

1893

January 9th School reopened this morning. Number on registers – 236, number present 154. The small attendance is due chiefly to the bad state of the weather and also to the fact that many are reported sick.

11th M. Heyhoe was presented at the close of the school with an album, a gift from the children and the teachers, on her leaving the school.

February 10th A candidate on Probation from the Girls Department is supplying the place of the ex Pupil Teacher.

March 25th [Extract from HMI annual inspection] 'III Class:- Reading and writing need special care; the children hold their books too close to their mouths, and do not speak out well. Small letters are well known, as tested by dictating – m, e, m, o, r, y, x, a, m, i, t, o, but the slates were dirty and the lines on them disregarded.

April 4th One little girl admitted this morning. Arithmetic taken by Class I instead of reading from 10.15 – 10.45 to avoid two reading lessons in the same room, classroom being too full to allow them in there anyhow. [Despite this overcrowding, children were still being admitted, including three 8-year-olds who had never been to school before. The lessons were changed around in an attempt to allow children the use of desks when most needed.]

April 25th Inspection by HM Inspector this morning. Numbers present 123 boys and 105 girls, total 228.

28th Number on register – 266.

May 5th 14 children admitted and one re-admitted. 98 children drafted to the Upper Departments, 47 were girls and 51 were boys. According to the wishes of HM Inspector, all children over 6 years old age (who could do their work) were included in the draft. These were sent owing to the great number on registers, and the fact that the average attendance (viz. 176.2) for the year 1892–3 exceeded the average for which the school is built (viz. 171). Number on registers – 182 (at present). Average this week – 172.3.

9th A holiday given tomorrow being Swaffham (May) Fair.

19th Number present – 183.

June 16th Several children absent through mumps or chicken pox.

Summary of HM Inspector's Report: 'In spite of the crowded condition of the school, the discipline is excellent. Excepting a few backward children many of whom have not been long in the school, all classes are well advanced. Musical drill is very good.' [In a special report on the premises HM Inspector remarks that the Offices (toilets) are too close to the school, and in his opinion, unsanitary. 'This matter should have attention at once.' He adds that 'Apex ventilation is wanted in the school,' and that the 'cloak room accommodation for Infants is insufficient.' The special attention of managers is requested to the enclosed Form 69. 'I am to point out that the average attendance in the Infants' Department has exceeded the number (170) for which the premises provide.']

23rd Many children are absent suffering from Mumps. Four have been sent home because of this.

July 5th School closed till Friday morning the 7th inst., to celebrate the wedding of Prince George & Princess Mary. The children of Swaffham are being entertained by Mr. F. Morse to tea in the Brewery Malthouse.

7th Only 88 little ones present this morning, small attendances probably owing to the festivities being kept up till rather late yesterday evening.

School closed this afternoon, for an indefinite period, owing to an order from the Sanitary Authorities – to close for one month; which period ends with first week of Harvest holidays, & no fixed date can be given for the re-opening of school.

September 4th School re-opened today.

8th Attendance is not good considering the number on books, 174 only being present out of 209.

After the long vacation the lower classes are backward in reading, the upper divisions have gone back greatly in writing.

October 13th Not a few children have skin diseases, and must be absent through this.

20th Mr. H. Day visited the school at 4.30 to say that a stone, new lamps and stones for the entrance to front door, would be provided, this being sanctioned by the committee at their last meeting.

27th The vicar and Mr. W. Plowright visited the school to ascertain what arrangements should be made for building new cloakroom, and putting in new apex ventilators.

November 2nd A child was sent home because his hands are peeling, and he shows every sign of having had fever, his mark cancelled from register.

10th School visited on Tuesday by two of the Sanitary Authorities who gave notice of the probability of closing the schools shortly, partly on account of sickness, and partly because of deficient sanitary arrangements.

1894

January 12th Because of the very bad weather, the playground is still in a very wet condition although the entrance has been paved, and shingle laid down beyond this.

March 8th In the playground the water has quite overflown the entrance owing to heavy rain, but some planks will be placed for children to cross over on going home. Meantime use has been made of a ladder which was laid down before two o'clock and children led across by teachers.

April 6th New registers commenced on Monday morning. Number on books boys – 121; girls – 103, total 224, admissions 6.

13th On Monday and Tuesday over 200 children present and on the Tuesday morning there was 205 – highest attendance made during the year.

24th Number drafted to upper department, in total, 76.

June 6th Remark – My Lords learn with regret that the defects of the premises pointed out last year have not been remedied and have hesitation in allowing a grant in the circumstances. They most urgently call upon the Managers to effect the proposed improvements at as early a date as possible.

September 14th During the holidays (August 2nd – September 8th) a new cloakroom has been provided, improved sanitary arrangements affected, and good ventilation in both rooms secured, by means of apex ventilators, and two extra panes of glass in each window being made to open in a slanting direction. A good water supply has been added.

October 17th Measles, Whooping cough, colds, coughs and sickness in many families meant that only 28 children were present. School closed by order of the Sanitary Authorities for one month.

November 19th School reopened today. Number present morning 118, afternoon 125. 40 above the age of five years still absent.

1895

January 28th Owing to very heavy fall of snow, only 22 children came this morning, and in accordance with the Vicar's wish, registers were not marked.

Games marching and singing were taken, and the little ones would have been sent home at 11 a.m., but as the snow fell so rapidly, were kept till parents came for them. In the afternoon only 12 came, and only one boy (who was carried by elder brother) had dry feet, the others stayed ten minutes, and were then sent home.

29th Only 48 children present, registers not marked, and marching, singing and recitation till 10.40, when they were dismissed. Owing to intense cold, it was difficult to keep even this small number warm. Only 57 little ones present again this afternoon, registers not marked after referring to Mr V. Smith, who said they were not to be marked till 60 children came. Those present, the elder ones, had musical drill the remainder looking on, and dismissed at 3 p.m.

30th a.m. Only 53 present, as snow continued to fall at intervals, it was thought best to send them home between the storms, all were therefore dismissed at 10.10.

p.m. 66 children present this afternoon, registered marked and closed by 2.30.

31st a.m. 58 children present, the wind being piercingly cold and very heavy snowstorms have fallen at intervals from 9.30 to 1.00. Registers marked and closed by 10.00 a.m. because of the rule for number of times school should be open.

p.m. 52 present, another snowstorm this afternoon, but after little ones were here, registers marked and closed by 2.30 p.m.

February 1st The teachers have stayed at school each day (with exception of Monday) until after the usual school hours were over.

28th Registers marked and closed by 9.30 a.m. dismissal at 11.30, so as to have rehearsal of Entertainment (to be given in the Assembly Rooms tonight) at 12 o' clock. (Singing and Drill were rehearsed).

March 1st Attendance has greatly improved this week, average 25 higher than that of last week.

April 5th New registers commenced. Number on books – 196.

26th Two children over six years of age and one over 5 years admitted, all had not been to school before.

May 7th Holiday given tomorrow because of Swaffham May Fair.

10th One boy of seven years admitted, who had not been to school before because of weak eyes.

14th The Education Dept. sent the following notice:- 'My Lords have sanctioned, on the special recommendation of Her Majesty's Inspector, the omission of the annual inspection of your school due in April 1896.'

17th A holiday given this afternoon. No absentees reported because so many little ones are suffering from colds and coughs and the weather today has been exceptionally cold and wet.

31st Summary of HM Inspector's report: 'Owing doubtless to poor attendance the children are less attentive in class than they should be.'

June 21st Average attendance poor for this time of year. On books 156, average only 118.6.

July 16th School closed tomorrow for the July Fair.

19th One girl from the Union Workhouse left for Sporle [possibly 'apprenticed' in housewifery, i.e. a maid].

Harvest Holiday August 2nd to September 9th.

September 13th Six admitted this week. One, G. W. Wilson, was seven years of age last March, but never having been to school, knows only a few letters.

October 1st A small attendance this afternoon owing probably to closing of Boys' and Girls' School because of funeral of late Canon Winter. [A later entry states the closure was to allow choir boys to attend the funeral.]

December 19th to January 6th 1896 Xmas holiday.

1896

January Two admissions are very backward, being 5 and 6 years of age, but never having been to school before.

March 26th School dismissed at 11.30 to allow rehearsals in the Assembly Rooms.

April 1st New registers commenced. Number on books – Boys 90; Girls – 93; total 183.

27th A holiday given this afternoon in all three departments, instead of the usual one on Friday afternoon after inspection, as a Circus is visiting the town, and an afternoon performance for children is advertised.

May 12th School will be closed tomorrow (Wednesday) being Swaffham May Fair.

21st May General Report. The school fully maintains its high standard. The most noticeable feature is the perfect discipline and order. The repetition said with remarkable distinctness and accuracy for such young children. (Francis B. Champion)

July 14th School closed till Thursday July 16th for Swaffham July Fair.

30th June Copy of Summary of Her Majesty's Inspectors report for year ending March 31st 1896: Infants' School 'conducted with energy, diligence and success. Children bright and happy and evidently well cared for.'

July 31st I, Miriam J. Spires, resign my charge as mistress of this school today.

September 7th I, Annie J. Callcott, commenced my duties as mistress of this school.

21st Mr. Barrie came to the school arrange about a Penny Bank. Three children joined.

December 18th Miss Overton, formerly Assistant Mistress, left on the 30th November, has helped during the week, and was on Friday the recipient of a handsome gold brooch presented to her by the teachers and children of the school.

1897

January 20th to 29th Attendance very poor and children sent home.

February 3rd In the night a very heavy fall of snow made the roads almost impassable.

12th Attendance very greatly improved.

25th February Head Teacher – Annie Callcott

Dimensions of School Room:
Large Room Length 48ft Breadth 20ft. Height 14 ft.
Class Room Length 24ft. Breadth 17ft. Height 14ft.

March 18th **The Vicar visited on Wednesday Morning, again on Thursday, and again on Monday and Tuesday morning.** [This was regular, as the Church had a heavy influence on the schools at this time. The Vicar took Scripture Lessons and the Diocesan Inspector also called at regular intervals.]

26th **The attendance is not so good, owing to bad colds and coughs amongst the children.**

27th **New desks were fitted in the school on Saturday.**

31st **Head Teacher resigns today.**

April 1st **I, Louisa Tilney, commenced duties as mistress of this school.**

April 2nd **Average for week, 128.**

9th **Work is being carried on according to a new timetable as a test.**

21st **Classes are still working to the new timetable. Gallery Lessons for 1897–8: Natural History: Mole, Fly, Silkworm, Frog, A Fish, Pigeons, Thrush. Objects: Coal, A Slate, Leather, Cork, Tea, Apple, Orange, Milk Water, A Shilling, Hen's Egg, Butter. Plant Life: Leaves, A Growing Plant, Wheat, Potato, Summer Flowers. Miscellaneous: Harvest Time, Baker and Bread Making, Postmen, Spring, Summer, Snow and Hail.**

29th April **Transferred children to Boys' and Girls' School.**

May 6th **Average 95.**

12th **Holiday given all day being Fair Day.**

June 14th **Reopen School after Whitsun Holiday, 119 children present.**

18th **Holiday given, Jubilee Week.**

28th **Open School after holiday. HMI Report from 28th April visit: 'The Infants' School will, I think, do well under the present teacher. Too much simultaneous answering is permitted. The First Class is too large and might form two divisions.'**

Staff: **H. L. Tilney** *Head*
      M. Josh *Article 50*
      E. Sear *pupil teacher fourth year*
      E. Kenny *pupil teacher fourth year*

Diocesan Inspector's Report: 'The school may be classified as good yet it appears to me to have fallen off to some extent, both in attention and Religious Knowledge since the last examination. This can be no fault of the present mistress, who has only been in the school a month.'

December 11th Head Teacher absent with Vicar's permission. Granville Smith visited for the first time.

1898

January 10th Number present 126.

February 8th Writing by far the weakest part of instruction, after examinations.

March 9th HM Inspector visited this afternoon. This is the second surprise visit this year.

Collective Lessons for 1898-9:
Natural History: Cow, goat, sheep, frog, bird, bee, silkworm, spider, feet of birds.
Plant Life: A Primrose, buttercup, growing seeds, how seeds are scattered, evergreen trees, wild flowers of spring, wild flowers of summer.
Miscellaneous: A candle, cotton, lead, a street, building a house, carpenters, farmyard, Spring time, Summer time, circle, oval, ring, common colours.

April 25th Transferred 32 boys and 33 girls.

May 20th Report of HM Inspector: 'The school is taught with much energy, and the children are attentive and well employed. The faults noticed in first visit have been attended to.'

Staff: H. S. Tilney *Head*
          M. Josh *Article 50*
          E. Sear *Article 68*
          A. Coe *Pupil Teacher 2nd Year*

General report of Diocesan Inspector: 'The school quite maintains the high standard of merit, which it attained under the direction of Miss Spiers.'

July 1st Average for week 139. This is somewhat low, as there are 177 on books.

December 7th Vicar visited this morning and as there were only 40 children at school, out of 199, registers were not marked.

1899

January 9th Opened school after Christmas Holiday. Only 87 children present, many away with Whooping Cough.

20th Average 76, this is due to so much illness.

26th Average 64, still much illness amongst the little ones.

February 9th Average only 55 children.

17th Average is now 81 children.

24th Average is now 99 children. Many children are still away through illness.

March 17th Average for week 121.1.

24th Average for week 79 owing to deep snow.

April 17th Transferred 38 girls and 30 boys to upper departments.

27th July Report of HM Inspector 1899: 'The Infants are being taught with much brightness and animation, and are making very gratifying general progress. The gallery in the classroom should be furnished with suitable desks.'

October 16th Half-holiday today for children to attend the ceremony of the Laying of the Corner Stone of the new Girls' School. (By Miss Amherst)

December 15th School closed for 3 weeks owing to Mumps.

1900

January 15th Number on roll – 174, but a great deal of sickness, causing so many to be away that the school was closed.

17th Mistress returned after sickness, average attendance of pupils for the week was 90. Much illness still prevents many children coming to school.

14th February Only 8 children came this morning in snowstorm. These were not kept.

15th Owing to fast-falling snow only 30 children came, and these wet and cold, School not opened.

March 2nd Average attendance 116.

April 2nd Transferred 50 children to girls' and boys' schools.

20th School closed for a week for bazaar.

24th Half holiday to celebrate relief of Mafiking.

List of lessons for year ending March 31st 1901

Animal Life: Frog, Cat, Donkey, Fox, Sheep, Robin, Spider, Butterfly, Animals tails and their uses, Herring.

Plant Life: Bean, (a) Growth of seed, (b) description of plant, A fern, a tree, tea.

Objects: Coal, (a) properties, (b) how obtained (c) uses, Gold, A Window, Envelopes, A train, a pond, an egg.

Miscellaneous: Soldier, Sailor, Sweep, summer, Winter Autumn.

July 18th Holiday given as usual being Fair Day, many children have chicken pox and the average is low 120.

September 21st Average for week 154.

October 3rd Edith Hawes began work as monitoress.

October 19th Half-holiday given on Thursday afternoon, it being the day for Dedication of the Bells.

1901

Report of HM Inspector 1900: 'The Infant are obedient and attentive and are making very satisfactory progress in their work.'

Staff: H. S. Tilney *Headmistress*
          M. Josh *Cert. 1st year*
          E. Sear *article 50*
          A. Coe *Pupil teacher 4th year*

March 29th School Year ends, average 128.

April 1st **23 Boys transferred to Boys' Department and 27 Girls' transferred to the girls Department.**

April 9th **After Easter Holidays, only 84 children present.**

May 9th **Copy of HM Inspector's Report: 'The Infants are being taught with much spirit and ability, and they evidently enjoy their school Life.'**

A. Coe has obtained Class II in Scholarship Examination (after attending a series of University Lectures) [Left school 20th September 1901]

June 28th **Mr Plowright (school manager) visited this afternoon & watched children at work.** [A steady trickle of visitors is recorded as disrupting the normal lessons. Another visitor and school manager was Miss K. Wilson, sister of (later) Admiral Wilson VC.]

17th **Holiday given, it being Fair Day.**

18th **Holiday this afternoon for School Treat.** [No description of treat, as Mr Pheasant would do in the Boy's School log books, as we shall see later.]

September 19th **School has been in charge of Miss Josh, as Mistress has been away through illness for four days.** [No entries by Miss Josh though.]

December 6th **Attendance much lower this week, as many children have measles.**

13th **Very many children away through illness.**

20th **School closed for fortnight Christmas holiday. School closed three extra weeks for measles.**

1902

January 27th **Opened school, only 42 present, owing chiefly to the weather.**

February 21st **Average this week very low 105. This is owing to coughs and colds.**

April 1st **Transferred 31 girls to girl's school and 38 boys to boys' department.**

Miss Minnie Josh is recognised as Certificated teacher.

25th **Percentage much lower (80%) several children have chicken pox.**

Copy of HMI Report 1902: 'The children are in very good order and they are well taught, but their progress has been hindered and the teachers' difficulties have been increased by the irregular attendance arising from sickness. The desk accommodation should be increased. E.L. Hawes is recognised under article 33.'

May 9th Average this week only 95, on books 138, many are suffering from measles & chicken pox.

26th Many children still have measles and chicken pox.

30th Attendance very small in consequence of measles and Chicken pox.

June 2nd Half holiday given in commemoration of proclamation of peace.

20th School closed for Coronation Week.

December 1st Admitted Florence Starling, a child of six who does not know her letters.

5th Attendance very poor owing to sickness and the snowy weather. Percentage 75 & 40. (Morning and afternoon)

1903

Jan 6th Opened school after Christmas holiday, very poor attendance owing to Whooping Cough, 71 present out of 163.

9th Percentage this week 47. This is owing to Whooping Cough and measles.

12th Admitted Dorothy Green aged 6 years who have never been to school before.

16th Percentage 45 owing to measles and whooping cough..

26 & 27 Admitted two children, one who has never been before and the other knows little.

Feb 26th Admitted another child, aged 6½, who has not been to school before.

March 31st School year ends – average 115.

April 1st Transferred 34 boys to boys' department and 28 girls to girls' department.

April 27th Admitted a child of seven who has never been to school before.

Copy of HM Inspector's Report: 'There has been an unusual amount of sickness among the Infants during the latter part of the school year. The teachers, however, continue to work with much zeal and earnestness and the general level of the work is, in the circumstances, very creditable.'

June 12th Average 104, many away with ringworm and chicken pox.

July 10th Average 102, on the books 145. Many are away through chicken pox and ringworm.

September 24th Admitted one child of six years who does not know her letters.

December 18th Attendance improved, although some few are away through illness.

1904

April 5th Admitted a seven yr old child who has always been too delicate to attend school.

18 Admitted a child of 6½ who has never been to school.

September 15th Sent in requisition for Pupil Teacher and School.

November 11th Mistress away this afternoon to meet chairman of Education Committee at Lynn. Miss Josh in charge.

Swaffham Infants' School, 1904.

1905

March 14th School closed for rest of week for colds and sickness.

20th School opened this morning with 116.

29th Received this day new books, new slates, new blackboard etc. from Jarrolds.

April 1st Transferred 22 girls and 27 boys to senior departments.

7th Only 47 children present owing to snow.

May 26th Several children are suffering from whooping cough.

30th School closed for rest of week for whooping cough.

June 5th School opened, 76 present.

7th Prizes distributed this afternoon by the vicar. Many parents and friends were present.

19th Opened school after holiday with 96 present out of 135.

July 5th Mr Parkinson, HMI visited and stayed a short time only. His wishes for the removal of the gallery have been carried out.

September 11th School opened after holiday. 134 present.

1906

February 2nd Daisy Newdick paid as a monitor from February 1st. [This is the first record of a monitor being paid.]

April 2nd 22 boys to Boys' school and 22 girls to Girls' school.

27th I H. Louisa Tilney resign my charge of the school as headmistress.

May 1st I, Fanny Taylor, take charge of this school today as headmistress.

4th Number on roll 119, average 105.

11th Number on roll 123, average 109, percentage 89.

25th The prize distribution took place yesterday in the Market Place. The Infants took five medals and thirty prizes. Number on roll 125 average, 111, percentage 89.

September 28th Miss Sear still absent from duty owing to the operation on her eye, which she has undergone. No supply teacher has yet been sent, though one has been applied for and this consequently makes the work difficult. Number on roll 141, average for week 122.

October 2nd Miss Oswell, uncertificated supply teacher, commenced work in this school this afternoon in place of Miss Sear.

October 12th Quarterly cards distributed, 58 (for good attendance)

November 9th A holiday was given on Monday, on account of the King's visit to Lynn. The attendance has been again very poor this week on account of the very wet weather.

22nd Miss Oswell, supply teacher left today and Miss Sear returned to duty.

December 7th Number on roll 147, averages for week 123. The under-fives cause the low average, as many whose names are on the roll do not come at all.

14th A holiday was given on Monday for attendance for October and November.

1907

January 18th to March 8th was a time of much sickness generally, much absenteeism.

April 8th Transferred 54 children to senior departments.

12th 30 new children have been admitted this week. Average 119.

19th Attendance has been very good this week – average 124, percentage 91.

April 16th Diocesan Inspector's report: 'The Infants School is thoroughly well taught, the children being very bright. A very good school.' Signed J. Wynne Davies

April 17th HM Inspector's report: 'The Infants are brightly taught and in good order. Some nice bold work in free arm drawing is being done, this, however, is carried out rather under difficulties – a blackboard, suitable for this work, fixed to one of the walls, would be a great boon. Frequent short exercises in voice production would be beneficial.

'Since the removal of the gallery from the classroom, this room has afforded ample floor space for full movement, it is to be regretted that very little space in the main room is available for this purpose. The system of ventilation is not satisfactory. The floor needs attention in places and the nails should be punched down.' Signed Rev. M. Blockley

[The comparison between the above two reports shows HM Inspector is more concerned with the material fabric of the building, as opposed to the Diocesan Inspector's interest in the spiritual well-being of the children.]

May 17th The Prizes and medals to be distributed at 3 p.m. by Mr Blockley – 37 prizes and ten medals. Average for the week 122.

June 22nd A half-holiday was given on Thursday afternoon for the Temperance outing. Average 142.

July 14th Attendance poor again this week average only 134 out of 164 on roll.

November 22nd [A week of bad weather caused the attendance to fall.]

December 20th A good attendance this week, average 145. The children are having a Christmas tree this afternoon.

1908

January 31st The attendance has been very poor indeed this week, owing to sickness among the children average 98. Mumps is the main cause.

February 18th The school re-opens today after being closed for a fortnight. It was found necessary to extend the time the school was closed.

March 27th Attendance much improved with average of 132.

May 22nd One fresh case of mumps and three cases of measles this week.

May 29th Very poor attendance. Several more cases of measles have been notified.

June 5th School closed for Whitsuntide holiday and did not re-open until July 6th, owing to a bad epidemic of measles. 83 children present out of 154 on roll.

July 29th The distribution of prizes took place this afternoon on the Vicarage lawn, in the presence of parents and others. School closed for summer vacation.

23rd October By order of the medical officer five children from the Watton Road are excluded till further notice, owing to a case of scarlet fever.

November 6th The children who were excluded for the above reason have now been permitted to return.

1909

January 29th Average for the week 123. I Fanny Taylor, resign my charge of this school today.

February 1st I, Mary Alice Hornsby, take charge of this school today as headmistress.

May 24th This afternoon, at 2.30, the children proceeded to the Vicarage Grounds, and were presented with the prizes awarded for Religious knowledge and for regular and punctual attendance. (30 prizes)

July 8th A holiday given this afternoon for the missionary pageant.

September 21st I Bertha Death, take charge here today.

27th My temporary charge of this school expires this afternoon.

28th Headmistress returned to duty, this morning after being absent since Sept. 20th owing to bereavement in her family.

October 15th The medical inspection took place today, 43 children were examined.

21st Trafalgar Day was observed by the children marching round the Flagstaff, saluting the flag and singing the National Anthem.

22nd Holiday on Monday in honour of the King's visit to Norwich.

December 2nd Children assembled and registers marked at 1.30 this afternoon, to enable the teachers to attend 'story telling' by Miss Marie Shedlock.

1910

January 28 The average for the week 60.2. Inclement weather all week.

February 25th Stock taken of reading books and kindergarten materials.

May 9th Scripture Report: '"Charming" is perhaps the best word to describe the Swaffham Infants. They are so bright and eager, yet so well trained that their eagerness does not become too aggressive, which speaks volumes as to the patience, tact and teaching of the staff. The repetition in all the groups is most excellent. Perhaps there might be a little more "life" in the singing.' S. Martin Jones Diocesan Inspector. [There is seldom any criticism from the Diocesan Inspector.]

12th The prizes for regular and punctual attendance were distributed this afternoon by Mrs. Lee Warner.

July 7th, 14th & 21st. Half-day holidays for Sunday school treats and the local flower show.

September 19th School was reopened with 16 children admitted and 141 present.

30th Two shillings sent towards King Edward's Memorial Fund.

November 23rd Six pictures in oak frames were received from Jarrold & Sons as requisitioned in March.

1911

January 20 Average for week 130 with 170 on books.

May 3rd Two pictures framed in oak received also 34 books. Attendance prizes.

May 18th HMI Mr A. E. Kenny Herbert – inspection March 22nd 1911

Infants Premises: The attention of the managers is invited to the following points:-

1 In the main room, three classes are taught side by side. The only separation of the classes is by means of two green baize curtains, which do not prevent the distraction of noise, and make the middle section of the room dark. A

folding partition of wood and glass is very desirable.

2 The cloakrooms are barely adequate for the number of children present, the doors open inwards, the porch used by the second class is not ventilated, is rather dark, and in it the pegs are too close together. A separate exit should be made for the babies, who have now to pass through the main room.

3 On the day of inspection there were 76 children on the 'Babies' register. 58 were present. There are only seats for 50, and the accommodation of the room (measuring 25 feet by 17 feet) would appear to be 47. It is understood that this overcrowding is temporary – but it is hoped that children will not be admitted to this room so freely in future.

June 22nd The school closes this afternoon (for the Coronation Holiday) until July 3rd.

September 22nd The First Class Attendance reached 100% this week.

27th Miss Wilson visited this afternoon, heard children sing, watched them at expression work, also checked registers.

November 6th Attendance Officer called with form to be filled in, for proceedings against the parents of a child, who has made 37 attendances out of a possible 133.

November 13th Case against the parents of the child above, dismissed.

December 13th Checked the registers F.K.S. [Fredrick Keeling Scott]. The north end of the big school is cold. At my request the temperature was taken upon three days, with this result –

> Dec. 6th At 9.00 a.m. 41 Degrees [Fahrenheit] at 12 noon 44 degrees.
> Dec. 7th at 9.00 a.m. it was 41 degrees again and 12 noon 45.
> Dec. 8th at 9.00 a.m. it was only 37 degrees.

15th Several wet days this week which have caused reduction in attendance.

1912

February 23rd The children, whose parents signed permission papers, attended Church on Ash Wednesday (about 100).

April 15th **20 boys and 36 girls were transferred to upper departments.**

Staff for year 1912–13:   Mary Alice Hornsby *Certificated Head Teacher (Class I)*
Margery E. Coe *Certificated teacher assistant Class II*
Emma M. Sear *Uncertificated assistant Class IIa*
Minnie Josh *Certificated teacher assistant Babies*

May 9th **63 books for prizes received from Norfolk Education Committee.**

13th **48 chairs and 12 tables received for Baby Room.**

23rd   **Prizes for regular and punctual attendance were distributed this afternoon (63).**

June 18th **The following is a copy of a notice received this morning:**

I advise that the Swaffham School, Infants' Department be closed from June 18 to the 5th July inclusive on the following grounds:- Prevalence of whooping cough, the exclusion of individual children having failed to arrest the spread of the disease.

Signed J. T. C. Nash (School Medical Officer)

17/6/12

July 8th **School reopened 84 present in the morning. 136 on books.**

November 13th **A note was sent to a child's mother about his untidy and dirty condition (absent in afternoon).**

14th **The child mentioned above returned to school this afternoon in a much better condition.**

December 10th **The same child was excluded from school as he was suffering from scabies.**

13th **Good attendance this week 136.3 average.**

16th *a.m.* **Moore and Grimshsaw Esq., HMI came in for a few minutes to see the Christmas trees.**

19th **The usual lessons were left at 3.15 p.m. this afternoon and presents from the Christmas trees were distributed. Mr. & Mrs. Blockley, Misses Smith and Harbord, Mrs Scott & Mrs Bunting were present. The Rev. M. Heath took part as Father Christmas.**

20th Miss E. M. Coe terminates her engagement in this school at the end of the month.

1913

January 6th School reopened after the Christmas holidays. The excluded child returned to school, but as he was not better was sent home again.

February 14th The excluded child returned to school on Wednesday 12th after being absent since December 10th (medical certificate produced).

20th After communicating with Dr. Nash, the same child was again excluded on Monday 17th as he was not free from spots.

April 25th Two girls were excluded on Wednesday 23rd (for scabies).

May 1st Notice of closure was received from medical inspection branch, on account of measles.

Period of closure 1-5-13 to 9-5-13. Whitsun holiday follows this period.

Average attendance for week 88.

19th School reopened. 64 children present, 123 on books. Most of the absentees are suffering from measles. The excluded girls returned to school.

June 6th Two girls excluded from the 4th for scabies. (The same girls as above.)

11th The excluded boy returned to on Monday 9th but was sent home again as he was not free from scabies.

30 The excluded girls returned to school. This afternoon at 3 o'clock, the prizes for regular attendance were presented to the children on the vicarage lawn.

July 24th A half holiday this afternoon for the flower show.

September 2nd School was reopened this morning after the summer vacation. The holidays having to be extended a week, as the alterations to the building were not finished.

October 1st Dr. Parkinson examined 8 children who had adenoid and enlarged tonsils at the last medical examination. Only one child has been operated upon.

3rd The alterations to the school consist of a window in the main room in place of the front door and porch. South window in the Baby room has been removed to the West Side, a cloakroom has been built at the back of the main room, and the whole of the school has been colour washed and painted.

November 17th A half holiday was given this afternoon to allow the scholars to visit Bostock's Menagerie.

19th Two framed pictures were received from Boots Co. Ltd.

28th A curtain for the main room was received from Chamberlins Ltd. of Norwich.

December 18th The usual work was abandoned at 3 o'clock and the presents from the Christmas trees were distributed to the children. The Rev. D. N. Heath was acting as Santa Claus. Many parents and friends visited the school during the week to see the Christmas trees.

19th School closes for the Christmas holidays.

1914

January 23rd Two pictures (framed) were received from Jarrolds on Tuesday.

February 11th Four children were excluded from school this morning, for dirty heads. N.C.C. Nurse visited the school on Monday.

16th Two more children excluded for 'dirty heads'.

27th W. E. Grimshaw and A. Johnson Esq. inspected the school today.

May 4th Report by HMI Mr. W. E. Grimshaw Inspection February 27th 1914. Much good work is being done. The children have a happy time, and those in the lowest class are particularly bright and friendly. The teachers are interested in their work, and do not spare themselves in their efforts for the benefit of their scholars, though in certain points of detail, discussed in the school, the methods employed might be improved. It would also be an advantage if slightly different arrangements were made for the instruction of those children who come to school for the first time when comparatively old.

21st The prizes, 27 in number, for Regular and Punctual Attendance were distributed on the Vicarage Lawn this afternoon. A large number of parents and friends were present.

June 23rd After a medical examination, two children were excluded. One had Scabies, the other had ophthalmia (conjunctivitis).

July 3rd The attendance has fallen during the week. Sickness is being prevalent amongst the children owing to the heat.

July 22nd There will be a holiday tomorrow as several Sunday school treats are being held.

October 2nd There has been an improvement in the attendance this week. The first division of class I made 100%.

19th Miss Josh absent today, to visit her brother who is going to the Front.

November 13th. The attendance has fallen considerably this week. Children are suffering from colds etc. One case of scarlet fever.

December 22nd Presents from the Christmas tree were distributed at 11 o'clock this morning. School closed for Christmas holidays this afternoon.

1915

January 29th Children assembled at 1.30 this afternoon and were dismissed at 3.30, in order to enable the cleaner to begin her duties earlier as it is not desirable to have lights in the school buildings after 5 p.m.

February 26th An exceeding low attendance this week. 29 children have been absent the whole week. Coughs and colds are prevalent.

May 31st 15 book prizes received this morning for punctual and regular attendance.

June 11th Several cases of whooping cough reported to M. O. H. this week.

July 1st The Head Mistress was out of school this afternoon for about ¾ of an hour to attend the funeral of the late Mr. Culling, a former manager of the schools.

5th Miss Culling returned to school this morning.

6th The prizes for regular and punctual attendance were given to the children this afternoon at 3 o'clock, on the Vicarage lawn in the presence of a number of parents and visitors. The prizes were 15 in number.

16th Several children away with Whooping Cough.

September 17th Eleven scholars have been admitted this week. Average attendance for week 108.6.

October 1st The average for the week is 106.4. Very bad coughs are prevalent amongst the children, and the attendance has therefore suffered.

November 1st The children are dismissed at 11.45 a.m. and reassemble at 1 p.m. to 3 p.m. This arrangement is to be carried out until the end of January, to enable the cleaner to perform her duties by daylight.

1916

January 10th Miss Culling's engagement in this school terminated on December 31st 1915.

11th Nurse Bullock visited this afternoon and examined the ringworm cases.

February 4th Average for the week 123.7 (145 on books).

March 2nd A half holiday is given by the managers this afternoon to allow the staff and some of the children to attend the funeral of Mr. Blockley, late correspondent of the schools.

24th This morning a 'Notice of Closure' was received from the Medical Officer of Health, on account of an 'Epidemic of Measles', from March 24th to April 14th.

May 1st On Sunday April 16th, notice was received from the Medical Officer of Health that the school would not be opened until after the Easter Holidays owing to the prevalence of measles. Duties were therefore resumed this morning. 16 children absent. 49 children were transferred to the upper departments.

24th At 3-o-clock this afternoon, in the playground, 29 certificates were presented to children who had made 95% of regular and punctual attendances during the year ending March 31st 1916.

August 8th A letter and a ringworm pamphlet were sent to a parent this morning advising her that her child is suffering from ringworm. The letter was delivered by Miss Miles (student teacher). (A specimen of the child's hair was taken from affected part of head on Friday.)

September 28th A ringworm pamphlet was sent to the same child's parents as before.

1917

March 9th Two letters to the parents of two children were received from Dr. Nash, in reference to these children suffering from Ringworm. The letter to the first parent was delivered personally by the Headmistress. The letter to the other child's parents was sent as the headmistress had previously visited them.

Staff for the School Year 1917–18:   Mary A. Hornsby *H.T. (C) Class I*
Minnie Josh *(C) Babies Class*
Emma M. Sear *(U) Class II*
Hilda M. Miles *S.T.*

July 13th Very poor attendance this week owing to prevalence of mumps.

August 3rd There has been a very poor attendance this week, owing to the prevalence of mumps and the wet weather.

October 9th A ringworm pamphlet and exclusion certificate were sent to the parents of one child, from the County M.O.H. They were delivered to the mother by the head teacher at school.

1918

January 16th As there were only 27 children present this morning, out of 135 on books, owing to the deep snow, the registers were not marked. All the children who arrived at school were kept there and received instruction. 52 present in afternoon.

25th There has a fair attendance this week. Average attendance 117.4, with 134 on books.

February 11th Two letters received from MOH to the parents of two children of different families. These children are suffering from ring worm of scalp. These letters were sent to the parents by older children of the family, as both mothers were interviewed by the nurse on the 31st January.

April 29th The vicar visited and stated that the temporary headmistress was expected to take charge of the school.

May 1st Temporary Headmistress expected now reported by vicar as not coming.

6th I take charge of this school for a week during the absence of the Head Teacher.

C. M. Yarmer (supply) left on the 10th May.

13th Mary E Kidd takes charge of the school today in the absence of the Head Teacher [until June 7th].

June 12th 180 girls from the Girls' school, with their mistress and teachers were present with the Infants this morning 9.10 a.m. A picture was unveiled by the vicar – who gave a short address. The picture was presented to the school by scholars past and present in memory of the late head mistress Miss Hornsby, who died May 13th 1918.

July 1st At the suggestion of Mr Fear (Inspector) some children were moved to different classes because some classes were rather large having as many as 51 children on the book.

August 2nd Owing to shortness of staff, the children attending school have been divided into two groups for convenience. Average attendance 114.9.

6th Miss Brown of the Permanent Supply Staff, helps this week.

17th Morning school 9 a.m. to 11.30 a.m. and afternoon 12.30 to 2.30 p.m. to enable children to gather blackberries.

19th School opens same hours. Also on the 24th and 26th and October 1st and 3rd.

October 8th – 21st School closed owing to illness of staff and no supply teachers available.

24th Dorothy Jackson headmistress of Holt Infants' school, took charge of this school today, during the closure of my own school. [Left on 1st November.]

November 3rd Orpah Evelyn Turner takes charge of this school today as head mistress.

3rd School closed owing to influenza for a week.

10th School closed for another week. Only 40 children present.

December 6th Average attendance very poor, owing to influenza. No fires since Tuesday as no coal available.

1919

January 24th School closed for the day – no coal.

February 3rd No fires lit, physical exercises taken until coal arrives and fire lit.

March 6th No coal for afternoon fires.

June 30th A slight alteration was made in the afternoon lessons to celebrate the signing of Peace on Saturday.

July 14th Mrs Aldiss came and invited children to join Peace procession on 19th.

17th An alteration was made in the afternoon lessons for Peace celebrations.

August 5th Miss Coe and Miss McSweeney visited the school.

August 6th Mother Superior with two teachers from Convent and Miss Coe spent the morning in school.

September 22nd The school reopened, the inside has been painted green and light green colour washed.

One death has occurred during the holidays from whooping cough and ten cases reported.

October 10th Attendance falling owing to very bad colds, coughs and whooping cough.

31st School closed until November 10th for Peace Week.

November 10th School reopened and closed for three weeks for whooping cough.

December 1st School reopened. 82 children present out of 133 owing to whooping cough.

18th Miss Harbord brought her doll to show children in the afternoon. Mrs Bunting and Mrs Aldiss gave out Peace medals in the afternoon.

1920

January 5th Miss Josh sent in her notice on the first of January to take up Headship at Martham on the 1st February 1920. She left on the 31st January.

July 16th 51 absentees out of 109 on books due to measles, whooping cough and chicken pox.

19th School closed for two weeks for measles.

August 3rd School reopened 31 present as measles still raging.

4th School closed on August 6th for measles.

October 1st Miss Hamerton has sent in her resignation to take up a post in Derbyshire. (She started in May.)

November 11th Children went to church at 9 a.m. for Armistice service.

1921

February 21st A policeman called about a lamp window broken by children last Saturday.

March 8th A policeman called about a lost bangle.

May 23rd A boy, Philip Wright, aged 5, killed on the 13th. [No reason given.]

October 5th Money subscribed to buy a rocking horse for the school. Miss Turner went to the sale in the Assembly Rooms.

December 22nd Major Holmes came to school as chef for the Plum Pudding Feed.

1922

January 9th School reopened. The floors have not been scrubbed, the windows have not been cleaned, neither have the walls been swept.

13th Five cases of scarlet fever. Contact cases reported.

20th Average attendance reduced to 76 and the % to 60, owing to snowstorms.

27th Attendance still poor owing to outbreak of influenza.

February 21st Notice received from Mr. Daves, giving sanction to his Majesty the King's wish for February 28th to be a general holiday.

28th School closed all day for Princess Mary's wedding.

3rd March Attendance very poor on account of colds, influenza, scarlet fever.

April 11th W. Cole comes to school with letter from managers.

25th Miss Harbord visited the school & was shown the lavatories.

May 5th Vicar called and his attention was drawn to the state of school premises.

23rd Vicar visited and asked for Empire Pageant to be held on his lawn.

24th Empire Pageant held in the playground at 2.30 – 3.30 and ordinary school work stopped.

Miss Grimes invited to take photographs. [Viola Grimes was a photographer of note.]

December 21st **Major Holmes, Nurse Watts, Mrs Green and Miss Smith spent nearly all the morning with us. Vicar called in the afternoon to see Father Christmas.**

1923

January 28th **Vicar called about harmonium.**

April 26th School closed by King's wish for the Duke of York's wedding.

May 4th **Dr. Townend came again as Diphtheria is spreading.** [The Diphtheria outbreak was considered to originate in the old Baptist chapel next door to the school. In Swaffham Urban District Council records, there was no receptacle in the lavatory when the Salvation Army used the building.]

16th Dr Nash came in during the afternoon, examined all the children's throats, took seven swabs and excluded these pending results.

June 1st Empire Day celebrations in school in the afternoon. King and Queen's record to the children of the empire kindly presented by Mr G. Green.

28th School day reorganised to allow the dancers to take part in the garden fete on Miss Wilson's lawn.

August 4th Fathers' afternoon in school on Saturday afternoon to 'observe' (about 20 came).

October 15th Mrs Cockerton assaulted Miss Turner and case reported to Board of Guardians and committee.

December 10th School closed for one week for measles.

20th Plum Pudding served hot with custard at 11 o'clock. Major Holmes came as chef. Vicar came, also others. In the afternoon Father Christmas came at 2 o'clock (Mr J. Keeling-Scott.) All babies were invited to see Father Christmas.

1924

March 27th Captain Stainfield [a regular visitor] visited us in the morning. This is his last visit, he is leaving for Eastbourne. He left his address for the children's games to be posted on to him.

April 1st Twenty-four boys and sixteen girls transferred to upper schools. The previous Saturday afternoon the school was opened for the parents to see their work before being transferred.

May 23rd Empire Day celebrations in the playground.

May 26th The children who took in The House That Jack Built go on a shopping expedition with sixpence each, kindly given by Mr Jacobs [Treasurer of the Managers].

June 10th Dr. Nash visited the school in the afternoon, as whooping cough is prevalent, 77 present out of 104.

21st School closed for three weeks for whooping cough.

October 1st **Dr Sexton came for medical examination.**

10th October **Miss Larner removed (having only started on the 15th September)**

22nd **Dr Townsend MO and Mr Parry (surveyor) came to see drinking water. Sample taken by surveyor for analysis. Mr Jacobs came to see the broken desks in Class II.**

November 12th **Doctor Sexton and Mr Bullen visited the premises with Mr. Impson (builder).**

13 **Dr. Sexton called also Dr Nash and advised the schools to be closed for one day.**

21st **Dr Nash advises closure for today owing to epidemic of sore throats and fever.**

1925

February 4th **School closed until Feb. 13th for measles.**

16th **School closed until Feb. 20th because of measles.**

[The school opened and closed for 3 more times, on the 4th, 16th, 23rd, owing to measles and colds.]

March 9th **School opened, attendance very poor, 53 present.**

May 19th **Miss Turner absent, owing to motor accident.**

June 10th **Miss Turner started half-day duty until 22nd June.**

22nd July **Excerpt from HMI report: 'The more general activities were not seen on this occasion, but the scheme of training has been planned with care and good judgement. The school is appropriately used to a considerable extent by other teachers for visits of observation. In view of this, some simple form of individual records of progress to correspond with a broad grading of the apparatus used by the children would be of particular value.'**

7th September **School reopens after summer vacation. Miss Turner absent having medical advice to take a three-month rest.**

17th November Letter R.W. No.1 also a form of instruction were sent to the father of a boy in Lynn Street (the boy having Ringworm of the scalp). These were delivered by Miss Lauretta Newton, Student Teacher.

1926

January 11th School reopened after Christmas vacation, Miss Turner returns to duty.

10th November Miss Harbord called and left Poppies.

11th Armistice Day kept in school.

12th Two tuning forks been missing out of large room – one for a week, one for three weeks.

17th There was a sheet or Prayer Card missing.

25th Afternoon meeting began at one o'clock to allow children to watch funeral of one of our little scholars, Alfred Harris, accidentally killed by a car on 22nd 11th 1926.

1927

January 19th School closed until 28th inclusive for influenza etc.

February 17th School closed until 28th for whooping cough.

28th School reopened 56 children absent owing to influenza and whooping cough.

March 8th School closed for whooping cough until the 28th.

28th Attendance improved

June 2nd School closed for whooping cough until the 24th inclusive.

11th November Armistice Day kept in school.

23rd Miss Winter called about 'Pound Day'.

24th Children took their gifts after afternoon school to the Cottage Hospital.

2nd December Salary sheet missing. Brush found that has been missing since the 25th 11th 27. Miss Allison put on her hat and coat and went out in a temper just before 4 o clock.

December 5th She apologised.

1928

[Many teachers from other schools as far away as Tottington, for example, visited to observe teaching methods at Swaffham. These are usually teachers from village schools within ten miles. This was a common practice here.]

April 20th Miss Allison absent for interview at Whitehall for a post in Malay States.

June 4th Rev. Keeling-Scott came to wish the children goodbye as he is leaving next week.

July 2nd School closed for Prince of Wales holiday.

June 6th Salary sheet missing 2-12-27 found this afternoon in centre drawer of desk. The only time when the drawer was left unlocked was from 11 o'clock to 11.25, when I gave a lesson to babies. It is now necessary for me to lock every drawer and take the keys with me when I leave the large room. Parents' letters are also placed on my desk months after they should have been forwarded to the office.

July 11th The Government report has been received this morning. Inspected on March 26, June 20.

'Infants: The headmistress of this interesting and successful school has a clear conception of the purpose of modern aims and methods of educating young children and considerable originality. She has two intelligent and effective assistants and is herself a skilful teacher. Much of the apparatus in use has been made by the staff. There is no evidence of over-emphasis upon the rudiments of Reading, Writing and Number, but the standard of attainment reached in these subjects is, on the whole, decidedly above the average.'

1st August Medical notice forms found in envelope bag.

September 9th School reopens. Miss Allison and Miss Sear have been asked to co-operate with the head teacher to promote the harmonious progress of the school.

November 12th Miss Sear put on her clothes and went out of school 9.05 a.m. She returned bringing the vicar at 9.30 a.m. and both went away at 9.45 a.m. I refused to have the teacher back in school, until Committee gives permission.

26th Miss Allison returned to duty. Miss Turner will be absent having leave of absence.

27th Miss Sear returned this morning. [In red ink:] Miss Turner absent on sick leave. Miss Allison Acting Head.

1929

January 7th School reopens.

10th Miss Turner returns to duty.

[Entry in beginning and end of Infant's School Log Book by Miss O. E. Turner Head Teacher:] Owing to 'Irritation in School' see end of this book. Mr Reynish HMI suggested a fortnight's 'Leave of Absence' – 12.11.28.

15.11.28 Mr Read, County Inspector seconded Mr. Reynolds suggestion.

19.11.28 Dr Sexton informed me of 'Irritations being planned'.

25th – 11 28 Mr Moore [under secretary of Norfolk Education Committee] suggested I should see a Swaffham Dr. and get a MC. Not feeling ill, I refused so Leave of Absence was granted.

25.11.28 Sunday Mr Arnell [representative of the Education Committee and the National Union of Teachers, and possibly a friend of Miss Turner] offered Leave of Absence for 2 months & suggested I shall go at once to a place of safety & 'Irritation was planned' & might mean a long nervous breakdown. I refused to go until Tuesday.

26.11.28 At school in the morning & stayed at home in the afternoon.

27.11.28 Letter from N.U.T. & Mr. Darns – Secretary.

27.11.28 I travelled. At Swaffham Station a strange woman [Nurse Backhouse's sister?] with a yellow mark over left eye wished me 'Good Morning' & irritation followed me home, to Birmingham and beyond.

27.11.28 This is copied from Log Book.

28 The staff now consists of : -
    Miss Alison – Acting Head
    Miss Smith – C.A. Supply
    Miss Sear –   U.A.

? 12.28 I saw Dr. Suckling of Birmingham. Towards the end of interview he left me & entered dressing room & came out again with yellow mark over left eye.

17.12.28 A strange woman in Stourbridge approached me with peculiar marks on her face & stabbed me with hypo-needle. This caused a slight heart attack.

19.12.28 Letter received from N.U.T.

20.12.28 Miss Harbord gave it out in school that Miss Turner was very ill & would not be coming back for long time.

3.1.29 Letter from Mr. Moore asking when I should resume my duties.

10.1.29 I resume my duty

    Received   Jan. 16th 29

    Dear Miss Turner,
    I only painted with Iodine over my eye to cure a little rash. I'm
    sorry it frightened you.
    With kind regards,
    Yours faithfully,
    C. W. Suckling M.D.

21.2.29 In conversation with Major Holmes he said 'he had finished' playing practical jokes.

11th January Miss Allison did not give the information to her class as instructed to do so.

12th A boy was laid to rest in the cemetery. A wreath and bunches of flowers were sent.

11th March School closed for a week for influenza, colds.

May 1st Miss Turner absent owing to ill health.

June 7th The county inspector of school buildings visited the school.

19th An accident occurred in class II this morning. Teacher in charge was Miss Brown. A boy damaged his finger very badly in the desk, the boy was playing with the iron rest underneath, and was not due to any negligence on the part of the teacher.

9th September Following the resignation of Miss Turner, a new Head Mistress has been appointed to the school, her appointment commencing from October 1st 1929.

18th The teachers remaining on the staff of the school asked the committee, through the correspondent Major Holmes, if certain pages of the log book could be deleted owing to untrue statements made thereon by Miss Turner. The following is a copy of the reply from the committee.

> 19th June 1929 Major Holmes, Thornton House, Swaffham.
>
> Dear Sir,
>
> With reference to your letter of the 11th inst., I have to inform you that it is not possible to make deletions from the School Log Book. We are all aware that the remarks made against the teachers were part of the peculiar symptoms of Miss Turner's illness, and I think that if a statement were made in the Log Book, that Miss Turner had resigned her post owing to a nervous breakdown, it would not be necessary to take any further action. A log book is, of course, private, except for certain privileged persons, all of whom are aware of the circumstances under which the entries reflecting on the work of the teachers were made, and I am quite sure that it is not possible for these entries to do these teachers any harm.
>
> Yours Faithfully,
>
> H. Moore Assistant Secretary.

October 1st I, Alice Blamire, commenced duties as head of this school today.

14th Admitted 7 children from Cockley Cley school, that school having been closed.

1930

Jan 6th Miss Samples, Permanent Supply Teacher, sent to replace Miss Allison until an appointment is made.

9th Miss Blamire, head teacher, was ill in school today.

13th Letter from Miss Blamire informing us that she would be unable to attend school owing to influenza.

I, Olive F. Prouton, supply, commenced duties here today and am taking first class.

17th New reading books received.

February Head Teacher returned today. Miss Samples, supply, removed to the Girls school. Miss Prouton remains. No appointment of assistant teacher made yet.

March 13th Major Holmes called re moving the old seats and desks from the school premises. A little girl aged 5 has had her leg knocked and hurt by one of these old seats.

14th The little girl's leg is broken, but it was not knocked by the form, she slipped off the form, falling on her leg, thus breaking it. Attendance very low, owing to colds and coughs and 'pink eye'.

17th Dr. K. Williams and Nurse Welstead visited re Pink Eye – only three cases in this school at present.

19th The Rev. Barry Browne visited to say that there was to be a Manager's Meeting on the 19th re the appointment of an assistant teacher in place of Miss Allison who left December 31st.

24th Miss Olive Prouton commenced duty here today; having been appointed as trained certificated assistant in this school.

May 7th Mr. Read called 3.15pm. re new furniture.

June 12th Mr. Cairns, the school dentist, visited and examined all the children's teeth, and found that 29 children needed treatment.

16th Reported 5 cases of measles.

18th Received notice from MOH that the school should close from 19th to the 1st July owing to measles.

July 1st Reopened school 32 present out of 66. 17 fresh cases of measles reported to M.O.H.

4th Attendance this week 49% owing to measles.

30th School closed for one day – children's Sunday school outing to Hunstanton.

October 30th A boy was excluded for a week by Dr. Townend to be watched for signs of Diphtheria.

November 27th Closed for Thursday afternoon for concert rehearsal in the cinema.

1931

January 19th Received notice from Dr. Ruddock-West that Class I children must be excluded from today until the 23rd inclusive, owing to a case of measles having occurred in this class.

29th Mrs Lee-Warner visited school 11–12 a.m. and was very interested in the methods and work of the children and heard the Percussion Band.

May 1st Extract from HMI report: 'The former practice of retaining the children too long in this department has been discontinued. It is understood that records of individual progress and capacity are to be forwarded as one means of encouraging continuity in aims and methods between the Infant and the lower classes of the next department.'

May 6th

Staff: A. Blamire *Cert. Head*
          Miss Prouton *Cert. Asst.*
          Miss Sear *Uncert. Assist.*
          Marjorie Grimes *Pupil Teacher*
          Eveline Fitzmaurice *Student Teacher*

14th Ascension Day. The children attended Church 9 – 9.30.

June 8th A supplementary teacher in Lexham School spent the day here in order to observe methods of teaching, apparatus etc. [Pupil and Student

Teachers were often appointed for one term as part of their teacher training.]

July 29th School closed for Sunday school outing to Hunstanton.

December 4th Mr. Copeman visited and heard the children play their percussion band.

15th Half-a-day holiday in order that the children might practice their item for the Annual Sunday school Concert.

1932

January 18 30 children absent with coughs, colds and earache.

February 8th Sickness still prevalent 49 out of 70 children present.

23rd School closed for Measles from 23rd February – March 4th.

March 7th School re-opened with 44 children, 62%.

14th Permission is given to a girl (14 years of age) from the Girls School to come into the Infants School to observe Story Lessons. She hopes to become a Nursery Governess.

April 4th Re-opened school. Four admissions, making 74 on books.

11th Small fire occurred in the roof of the school, at the gable end over the south classroom.

19th Dr. Sexton visited to examine those children who have defect cards.

July 7th Report of Religious Instruction.

General Report

It is always a pleasure to inspect this school owing to the keenness of the children and their reverent behaviour.

The high standard of former years was fully maintained and the Infants are clearly receiving an excellent grounding in Religious Knowledge.

29th The dentist attended three days this week, and treated several children.

September 5th Re-opened school. Reported several cases of supposed Whooping Cough.

1933

January 23rd School closed from 23rd January to 30th January through influenza.

30th Extension of closure till Monday 6th February.

February 6th Further extension of closure till Monday 13th February.

13th School re-opened.

April 4th Harmonium tuned.

September 21st Several bricks from above the Baby Room window fell down last weekend. Workmen have been in school today to repair same.

1934

March 12th 27 children present out of 81. Dr. R. West ordered closure until Monday next.

19th School closed until today week.

26th March School re-opened.

August 2nd School closed for the Sunday school outing to Hunstanton.

3rd Many children absent today, not having returned to school after the outing yesterday. School closed for Harvest holiday.

November 29th Holiday given by the King, on the occasion of the wedding of HRH the Duke of Kent and Princess Marina.

1935

February 11th Milk scheme started.

May 3rd School closed for May 6th and 7th on the occasion of H.M. the King's Silver Jubilee.

14th Dr. Heslop visited re the water consumption and the lavatories.

July 3rd Received through Committee, through Mann Egerton & Co, one oak Cupboard and six oak dual tables.

9th Received 24 hardwood chairs.

September 26th A little girl, 5 years old, was knocked down yesterday afternoon by a car passing the school gate. She is not much hurt, having only a bruised knee. She is present at school again this morning.

November 6th Holiday given by his Majesty King George on the occasion of the Duke of Gloucester's marriage.

1936

28th January School closed on the occasion of King George V funeral.

31st School closed for the day, in order for the water drainage to be connected for the new lavatories, which are being installed for the Girls' and Infants' Schools.

February 24th Workmen repaired passage ceiling from which plaster had fallen.

March 17th Dr. Plattts called to discuss reorganisation.

23rd Mr. Fear called re National Savings.

April 1st I took over the Headship of the amalgamated school, Girls' and Infants', therefore, this Log Book is discontinued for the time being.

The Girls' School

Summary of log book entries 1863–1918

1860s

The number attending school on 29th May 1863 was very small, for it was Royal Oak day, commemorating the restoration of the monarchy in 1660 (it had been kept as an official public holiday until 1859).

As 11th June 1863 was St Barnabas' Day and the 24th June was St John the Baptist day, the girls attended church in the morning. Attending church on saints' days was a regular occurrence, but on Easter Monday and Whitsun Monday they attended church in the morning and only had the afternoon off. The vicar was a regular visitor to the school, sometimes taking lessons.

The log book at this time reflects the influence the Church still had on the children, a great many saints' days being recorded as reasons for attending church in the morning. Otherwise, most of the entries were 'ordinary progress'.

A new rule recorded on 11th September 1865 decreed that all attending the day school must attend on Sundays too. No penalties for non-attendance are listed.

On 16th March 1866 there was a special church service in the afternoon for the children to attend because of the cattle plague.

Miss Byass of the Manor House gave a present to every child in attendance in the morning on the 16th April 1868; the reason is unknown.

1870s

The ladies of the town, such as the Misses Winter and Montagu, frequently involved themselves with the school, taking lessons in singing and needlework, from 1871.

The school treats continued, but in 1875 the treat was cancelled until 28th January 1876, when a bazaar followed the tea, in which every child received at least one present. The next year, the annual treat was in August as usual.

Illnesses such as mumps and scarletina caused absences on many occasions. Occasionally there is a much more serious problem: typhoid fever is recorded as being the cause of the death of one young girl in December 1878. On 15th July 1879, the first reported cases of measles appear and this illness continued to cause considerable absenteeism until the school broke up for the harvest holidays on 22nd August.

1880s

The government inspector visited during June 1882. His report commended the girls for passing a 'very fairly good examination' and noted that 'grammar has been well taught on the whole', but criticises the handwriting for being 'too poor and cramped' (possibly because of the crowded conditions – this is not the first time this remark has been in the report). He also added that 'the results might be better if attendance were more regular'.

Mrs Pheasant, the wife of the headmaster of the boys' school, taught the girls. In 1882 their daughter, Amy, passed as a pupil teacher as did her sister Ethel.

Scarlet fever was still a menace in the town in September 1882, as four girls returned to school after the harvest holidays. The girls had been away for as long as nine months.

Absenteeism was common in a group of approximately 30 girls out of 148 in total; the names appear regularly as being reported to the Attendance Officer. The highest rate of absenteeism was 61 days away out of 118. The returns to the Attendance Officer had to be weekly and the teachers of all schools had to attend a meeting with the Attendance Committee twice, on 22nd January 1883 and 8th February 1883. In their own defence, at a meeting with the Vicar and the girl's Mistress, five girls made a statement to the effect that the Attendance Officer's wife told them to burn any Absence Enquiry Forms (as recommended by HM Inspector and agreed by the school managers). In addition to the pupils' names, the names of the parents ('where known') were added on the returns for 5th March 1883.

Attendance dropped generally because of the weather during the winter months because of the bad roads.

The ladies were still coming in to give lessons on darning, sewing and singing.

Even during the better weather in April and May, the absenteeism returns caused the Attendance Officer to visit the school frequently because of poor attendance by some girls. Illnesses such as sore throats caused some absenteeism, but the Mistress succumbed to illness because of overwork and was away in January 1884 and had to go to St Leonard's on the advice of her doctor. She was away until the 10th March. Mrs Jackson took her place in the meantime, staying until July of that year.

After church on 8th January 1885 a bun and an orange were given to each child in commemoration of Prince Albert Victor's 21st birthday.

Miss Strachan was not a good enough disciplinarian for the school: on the 24th July 1885 the managers were obliged to part with her because of this.

Miss Montagu's sewing lessons ensured that HM Inspector's report said, 'sewing is very carefully taught', but English lessons were not so highly praised. The emphasis on sewing (and darning) was because many families had to rely on home-made clothes, which were patched and repaired.

1890s

From early February 1890 until early March that year, influenza caused many children and teachers to be absent.

Admissions of children from small, private, 'Dame' schools were recorded. In March 1891 twelve children were admitted and eleven were 'scarcely fit for standard one'. The Inspector's report stated in May that 'all departments had suffered from large intake of backward children from the day and Dame schools', which had been superseded by state education.

On 21st September the managers resolved, during the holidays, to adopt the Fees Act and as a consequence, the schools were declared free.

Irregularity of attendance was reported in the log book and many children were reported to the Attendance Officer for being absent twice or more during the week. This was the enforcement of the 1880 Education Act. On one occasion 40 names were reported. During the harsh winters many children could not get to school; in February 1892, for example, 'very heavy falls of snow' were reported and no report of absent children was submitted because of the weather.

When the harvest began, 63 names were sent to the Attendance Officer, but the school broke up for the harvest holiday at noon.

Miss Montagu started a 'Penny Bank' savings bank in the school in January 1893.

The school closed for three weeks because of mumps in July 1893, shortly before the harvest holiday.

A list was given of occupations for girls leaving on 31st May 1894: domestic servant 6, helping at home 29, dressmaker 3, bad health 1, removed from the town 2, total 41. Number on the books – 216, all being taught in the upper floor of the school, still taught in accordance with the National School principles in one room using pupil teachers and monitors.

At this time, Mr Pheasant, master of the boys in the ground floor rooms, recorded that there were 203 boys on the books, making a total of 419 children in a school built for 350 which, when it opened, had 130 on the books. This 1894 total of pupils meant that the school was very overcrowded and sickness and contagious diseases spread very quickly through the packed classrooms.

A number of children were constantly absent, keeping the absence numbers close to 20 and above, unless there was sickness in the town, when the numbers rose and the reports back to the attendance officer were stopped for a while, until numbers returned to normal. One September, for example, all the schools were closed for a month because of the 'prevalence of measles' and 'the harvest not being finished'.

The Relief Committee provided hot soup on two days for the country girls who stayed for dinner in February 1895 because the weather was very severe.

The Sunday school treats of both the Baptist Church and Wesleyan chapel were responsible for absenteeism. The school treat is also recorded.

The school was still subject to persistent absenteeism with at least 16 and as many as 63 being absent on one day. On 15th November 1895 it was written, '16 of them are habitually away at least once a week'. This increased in March 1896 when '22 are habitual absentees'. The numbers slowly went down and single figure absenteeism, except during periods of illness, were common.

The Queen's Diamond Jubilee celebrations meant that the school broke up for a week's holiday in honour of the occasion. There is no other reference to the celebrations.

On 19th November 1897 some 33 habitual absentees were recorded and sent to the Attendance Officer.

The headmistress, Mrs Pheasant, had a bad attack of influenza from January 1898. She was so ill that she did not return until 25th April. On that day 33 children were admitted from the Infants' School, but no comment is made as to their abilities.

Miss Montagu, who was mentioned virtually every day as giving sewing lessons since 1871, is still there 27 years later, as is Miss Smith, who took singing lessons after Miss Winter. Both Miss Winter and Miss Smith were the daughters of Swaffham vicars.

Whooping cough caused much absenteeism in January 1897 and the next week chicken pox meant many were absent. It was not until March that the attendance figures improved. The redoubtable Miss Montagu and Miss Smith still did their voluntary work there, though.

On 24th March 1899, a notable addition to the timetable, sanctioned by HM Inspector, is elementary science. The lessons in this subject are listed and include plants, air and water in detail, as well as some manufacturing processes. However, the Inspector's report refers to History and Geography not being subjects on the timetable.

A notable remark in the Inspector's report was that the girls had to leave the building via a staircase and one door, only two feet eight inches (81 cm) wide at the top of the stairs.

On 16th October 1899, the foundation stone of the new Girls' School was laid next to the Infants' School in White Cross Road. The Honourable

Margaret Amherst (of Didlington Hall) laid the stone. All the children were present. The site of these schools was previously glebe (church-owned) land.

On 15th December, the school was closed by doctors' orders, due to the prevalence of mumps, which had caused absenteeism since 3rd November.

1900

In January influenza struck again, causing more absenteeism. It was not until 23rd February that attendance figures began to recover.

The girls had a week's holiday because of preparations for a bazaar in aid of the School Building Fund on 25th and 26th April.

The Relief of Mafeking and the Queen's birthday on 24th May meant a half-day's holiday.

The school reassembled in the 'New Room' on 11th June. Rev. Mr Norris conducted a short service, at which several of the managers were present.

All the girls attended an exhibition in the Assembly Rooms on 19th July. The subject was missionary exhibition in connection with the Society for the Propagation of the Gospel. There were many articles from foreign lands on display and addresses were given.

A half-day holiday was given on 19th October to commemorate the rehanging of the church bells, paid for by Mrs Day in memory of her husband, H. W. Day (of the Norwich and Swaffham Bank).

Geography lessons were given to standards 1 to 3 in place of the normal lessons on 2nd November. Another new lesson was the 'Object lesson', where objects such as a piece of coal were discussed and their origins explained.

Mrs Pheasant left the school on 20th December after 38 years as headmistress.

1901

Miss Laura Cushing started as headmistress on 1st January. Five classes and their respective teachers are listed.

On 1st March twelve new sets of books were received. These covered History, Geography and Domestic Economy, now taught in the school. The school garden was dug and planted with flowers brought from home. Pot plants were also bought for the school windowsills. There seems to be a lessening of religious subjects and singing.

On 26th April the school received chemical apparatus for the illustration of elementary science lessons.

One hour a week was given for exercise in military drill for the upper classes, under a government directive.

Curtains were put up between classes in the large room on 31st October and were considered a great benefit in securing attention. Pupil teachers were given 1½ hours every morning in order that they could study. Pupils from standard 1, who were preparing for pupil teachers' work, took their places.

1902

The school closed for two weeks in January because of a measles outbreak, plus sore throats and colds, reopening on 27th January, despite many children still being away through illness; on 31st January attendance was still poor.

In a detailed list of lessons, there was no reference to religious education, the lessons taught being Arithmetic, English, Geography, History, Elementary Science, Needlework and Drill.

A week's holiday was given on 2nd June in honour of the Coronation of Edward VII. The children had tea, sports, etc. on 26th June.

1903

Miss Annie Cushing started at the school on 2nd February.

An inventory of furniture etc. was included in the log book in June. An interesting part of this is the seating for the girls. Long, hard, wooden forms with desks, some 11 feet (3.35 m) long, others varying between 7 and 10 feet (2.1 and 3.0 m) in length. There were only six chairs, and only two tables for the teachers. There was a harmonium – very useful to accompany the singing when HM Inspector called – and three clocks. Teaching aids included 204 framed slates, 10 blackboards and easels, 11 wall maps and 9 scripture charts. (This is just a sample of the list compiled by Rev. Granville-Smith, 'correspondent'.)

On 1st October the school was taken over by the Norfolk Education Committee. (This was when Miss Montagu apparently stopped coming to the school after approximately 32 years helping to teach sewing and darning etc.) On 16th October the Committee offered a reward for improvement of attendance, which resulted in a 96% attendance on 23rd October – 'very much improved', as the Headmistress, wrote. The Head was obviously pleased with the improved attendance, as she gave a half-holiday on 26th November.

The head examined the whole school in the last fortnight before the

Christmas holiday in 1903, and 'found a great improvement throughout, with the exception of class 4'.

1904

170 girls were on the books on 11th January and the Head remarked on the 'good attendance on books'.

The bad state of the playground caused most drill lessons to be cancelled in the week ending 29th January.

A half-day holiday was once again given on 20th April for good attendance. This was the second of several such holidays this year. During the evening, and the following evening, the children gave a concert in the Assembly Rooms.

The Diocesan Inspector's report on 2nd June was very complimentary, with the tone and discipline of the school being excellent. This was repeated the next year. The next day, a copy of HM Inspector's report was received and was also complimentary with a reference to the 'increasing regularity' of attendance and 'credible progress' in the work and good behaviour of the girls.

A heatwave from 27th June to 8th July caused drill to be cancelled. A longer playtime was given on occasion.

1905

The Shirehall was the venue for cookery instruction from 11th April (government grants had been available for cookery lessons since 1883 and for laundry since 1891). Some 54 children saw a demonstration of cookery there on that morning, and in the afternoon three classes attended. Miss Shipley, a teacher from the Norwich School of Cookery, instructed all girls.

On 7th June medals rewarded perfect attendance by 14 children. Another 68 children gained prizes and certificates. The next day the children had a half-day holiday for regular attendance. A 'quarterly card' would have been issued to those in regular attendance. Those absent for some good reason such as illness were mentioned in the log book.

The general work of the school had improved in neatness, according to a comment in the Head teacher's report after she examined all the school over a period of 10 days ending 4th August.

1906

A cookery course for 54 girls took place in the Shirehall on 23rd February, under Miss MacKenzie. Sewing lessons were replaced by the cookery lessons. Miss A. Cushing attended cookery classes and passed a relevant exam in the subject. Later, her sister, the Head teacher, took the same course.

A very interesting list of lessons and their contents was written as the syllabus of work for this year. The sewing lessons included virtually every garment a girl or lady might wear, such as nightgowns, petticoats, chemises and drawers. Repairs were also taught. Nature Study too was on the timetable, which also included object lessons and domestic economy lessons.

On Empire Day (24th May) the children assembled on the Market Place, receiving attendance prizes. Patriotic songs were sung and the school managers made speeches on the Empire. In the morning the teachers gave lessons on the vastness of the Empire and the privileges and responsibilities of living in the Empire.

From 28th September 49 girls attended a fresh cookery course, which ended on 2nd February 1907.

A evening concert was given in the Assembly Rooms on 17th and 18th October by the girls, the proceeds (amounting to £11) being used to buy eleven pictures (chiefly India prints) for the school walls. Various garments made of calico were began by classes. Knitting, practice work and darning still continued one afternoon a week and mending by upper standards from 7th November.

Two girls, Norah Lane and Edith Cushing, were awarded Junior County Scholarships in December 1906. There were 50 scholarships and 256 competitors.

The Addison Temperance Readers were read once a fortnight by standards 6 and 7.

1907

HM Inspector's report arrived on 8th April and was critical in many aspects such as the fact that four classes were working in that room with a nominal attendance of 135 girls. The inspector recommended that a partition be placed in the room. The cloakroom accommodation was 'strained to its utmost limits'. The lavatory drain was stopped up, too. 'The main room of the girls department must not be habitually occupied by more than 120 scholars,' said the Inspector, 'the number for which it is recognised as providing accommodation.' The old desks still in use in the classroom were mainly to blame for defects in the girls' deportment. Later, though, on 16th April, the Diocesan Inspector reported that this was 'an excellent school all through'.

Half-holidays for attendances were still being given virtually every month, as well as prizes for regular attendance. There was also a half-holiday given for a Temperance picnic on 20th June.

Friday mornings became the time for Miss Winter to speak about missionary work.

The glazed partition recommended by the inspector was installed on 9th September, just eight days before another inspector called.

The school lunch break was shortened by half an hour from 4th November to enable children to leave at 4 p.m. instead of 4.30 p.m. during the winter months. This continued until 3rd February 1908.

The school closed on 20th December for the Christmas holidays.

1908

Cookery classes were held in the Shirehall (across the road) on Thursday and Friday each week, with 65 children attending.

On 26th April the Diocesan Inspector reported that 'this school deserves the mark Excellent'.

Friday mornings became the time for Prayer Book teaching by the Vicar (Rev. Frederick Keeling-Scott). This may be in place of the Temperance lessons referred to in the previous June.

An outbreak of measles caused the school to be closed for three weeks.

A list first appeared during June of children detained in the same class as the previous year. Reasons given included ill health, very bad eyesight, private school, ill fed, undersized and delicate.

Attendance medals and certificates were awarded on the Vicarage Lawn at 2.30 on 29th July; the school was then closed for the Harvest holiday.

The entry of 10th October included eight candidates for Labour Certificates. These certificates verified the girls' suitability for work, but two girls failed. Girls and boys under school leaving age had to prove their regular attendance and capabilities in order to be allowed to leave school for 20 hours a week in order to work.

HM Inspector visited on 19th September and his comments recorded on 10th October: 'There are no desks in the school suitable for the use of children in the lower classes.'

The entry for the results of the terminal (end of year) examinations shows a general improvement, but arithmetic was a weak subject. It is not uncommon to see arithmetic results criticised in this way. The new methods of teaching written work for the youngest girls are criticised too, the results being 'distinctly poor below standard 6'.

Religious tolerance was in evidence in a letter from the Norfolk Education Committee, which stated that children could be withdrawn from Religious Instruction on Ash Wednesday and Ascension Day if a letter was received on each day.

Staff turnover is always noted and many teachers leave to go on to better positions, often as the Head of another school.

A flagstaff was erected in the school playground so that the Union Jack could be hoisted in celebration of Royal birthdays and anniversaries of historical importance. The flag was first hoisted on 21st October and the children sang national songs and the National Anthem.

A day's holiday was given to celebrate the King's visit to Norwich in order to present new colours to the Norfolk Regiment and to open the new wing to the hospital.

A temperance lecture for all the girls in standards 4, 5, 6 and 7 was given; there were frequent visits by members of the Temperance Society to lecture on this subject.

1910

The Diocesan Inspector visited in May and reported that the school was 'Excellent'.

HM Inspector visited on 25th April, reporting that 'there is too much done for the children and as a result the Headmistress finds the girls "sleepy". There is want of interest, notably in arithmetic, but in all subjects generally, and there is little blackboard work.' Some lessons were said to be too long. A favourable comment was that 'Needlework in the top class is carefully taught, and the girls are making their own garments.' Other than that, the Inspector considered that the girls were not working things out for themselves. The older girls 'should be thrown more on their own resources. The school should be much improved.'

Elaine Cushing and Catherine Avis were successful in obtaining Junior County Scholarships. They were placed 7th and 15th in order of merit, out of 230 competitors for 40 scholarships.

A list of girls who were retained in the same class as before appears in April.

One girl eight years of age had never been to school before.

1911

Unusually, the Diocesan Inspector's report for 1911 was less praiseworthy than usual, criticising the paperwork in the upper standards, which he said was 'decidedly weak'. HM Inspector, on the other hand, was pleased with the improvement since last year, praising the lower classes and the top classes for their improvement. The middle section was said to be the weakest in the school, but there was hope that the new teacher would 'do much to improve the school'.

The school closed on 2nd June for the Whitsun holidays and on 12th June, five exhibits were sent to the Education Officers 'with a view for exhibition at the Royal Show'.

On 21st June the school closed for ten days to celebrate the coronation of King George V. Special and incidental lessons were given in the morning throughout the school. The next day children attended church in the morning and joined in the afternoon sports and had tea on the Antinghams at 5 o'clock.

There was a problem with one family, whose children were excluded on 15th September for a week because of being dirty. The children were later excluded for a further two weeks and eventually, on 13th November, the family was prosecuted. Warning letters were sent to the parents of two other dirty children.

The school purchased a piano, partly with money from a concert the girls gave in the Assembly Rooms and partly from a grant from the Education Committee.

The children purchased two fir trees which were planted in the playground to commemorate the Coronation of King George V on 23rd November.

The Shirehall was the venue for laundry lessons from 4th to 15th December, and again in November the following year. (This was while the Shirehall was still an active courtroom and police station, with cells.)

1912

East Dereham Secondary School for Girls opened on 24th January and four scholarship winners from Swaffham Girls who had been attending Miss Pegler's school now attended the new Dereham School.

A new cloakroom was added on 15th April at the south end of the school for

Swaffham girls in 1911.

standards 1, 3 and 4. Now each classroom has a door leading to the cloakroom.

Four girls left having obtained places in secondary schools, two in Thetford and two in King's Lynn. (These secondary schools were later known as High Schools.)

1913

The Diocesan Inspector came to call on 20th March and examined the girls. The 'answering was admirable, and the paperwork, very creditable'.

Certain girls were excluded on 18th April because they had not had measles, on order of the office. This was followed by closure of the school on 3rd May because of an outbreak of this disease.

Dr Campbell in the Shirehall held an eye clinic for cases recommended by Dr Parkinson during June.

When the school reassembled after the summer holidays on 15th September, there were 195 girls on the books.

The second pair of glasses to be given to girls was measured for, and given to, one of the girls. These seem to have been paid for by the Committee. This was in an age long before the NHS.

The first mention of the 'Local Care Committee' was on 20th October, when they had a meeting, presumably at school.

The dreaded 'Nit Nurse' first made an appearance on 7th November, although not under that name of course. She was back on 10th December and 29th January 1914, examining children's heads.

17th November was a half-holiday given for the visit of a menagerie (possibly Wombwell's).

HM Inspector reported on and was not pleased with the continued help given to the girls, but not so much as previously. As four years ago, he said that children should practise correcting their own errors. Children were being taught to use text books and maps in standards 3 and 4. The long 10-foot (3 m) desks were hampering the work of the lower standards considerably.

1914

On 24th June the sum of ten shillings and six pence was sent to the Cottage Hospital in aid of the Alexandra Day Collection.

Several cases of scarlet fever were reported on 6th November and Dr Nash examined suspicious cases and excluded three pupils. One classroom was ordered to be cleaned with 'Jays (sic) Fluid'. The school was closed on the Friday afternoon and some disused books waiting to be condemned by the County Inspector were immediately disposed of. These books had been lying around for seven months.

The first mention of the First World War was on 30th November, when the schoolchildren who had collected their pence over the past month sent the money, plus five shillings from the staff, to Princess Mary's Fund For Christmas Presents For The Troops. Twenty-eight shillings was sent to Buckingham Palace.

1915

On 29th January the school started opening at 1.30 instead of 2.00 to avoid having lights after 5 o'clock. Later, on 1st March, the school resumed opening at two o'clock, but closed at 4.30.

May Read was successful in gaining a Junior County Scholarship on 7th June being number 7 out of 321 competitors.

The annual prize distribution on 6th July was, as usual, on the Vicarage lawn and the band of the Sherwood Rangers was in attendance.

The school closed early on 22nd September to allow elder children and teachers to attend a special service at church in memory of Miss Mary Winter, a frequent visitor to the school. Miss Winter used to attend school to help girls with their singing.

Trafalgar Day was celebrated on 21st October, and a collection was made for the Red Cross Society. One guinea (£1.05) was sent to the headquarters. The children sent three sacks of potatoes to the Bilney Hospital for the Wounded. On 24th and 25th November concerts were held in the Vicarage Room by the school to provide comforts for the 5th and 9th Norfolks at the front. £10 profit was made. The girls wrote letters to many of the men and received grateful acknowledgements.

Lighting Orders made alterations to the timetable necessary from 1st November so that the school could close at 3.15 p.m.

1916

From 31st January the school closed at 4 p.m. (but again from 30th October the winter timetable enabled the school to close at 3.15 p.m.).

The girls gave an entertainment on the Vicarage Lawn in aid of the children in Belgium. The sum of £3 10s (£3.50) was made.

The girls gathered around the flag, saluting it and singing the National Anthem to celebrate Empire Day on 24th May. Lessons on patriotism were given during the morning. In the afternoon, prizes and certificates were given on the Vicarage Lawn.

The Diocesan Report was very favourable this year, commenting on the care and accuracy of the Gospel Hymns, the Commandments, and the reverence of the School prayers.

1917

Miss Cushing, the Headmistress, was absent due to illness from 29th June, returning on 7th January 1918. No reason is given in the log book, but photographs show Laura Cushing confined to a wheelchair.

The girls of the first class made 56 laurel wreaths for the memorial service in commemoration of the 56 men who had fallen. This was on 3rd August, a year before peace was declared and before the red poppy became the symbol of such sacrifice.

1918

War Savings Certificates were purchased as each child saved 15 shillings and 6 pence. This was recorded on 4th February; on 15th February Dr Jenkins spoke to the children about the War Savings Association to be formed in the town.

Accommodation of Girls School:

Area of Big room (55.75 x 21.5 ft)	1198½ sq.ft	Accom: 119
Classroom (21 x 19.5 ft.)	390 sq.ft	39
Classroom (21 x 19.5 ft.)	390 sq. ft	39
	1945 ½ sq.ft	Total 197

Extracts from the log books 1918–45

1918

Staff: **Miss Laura Cushing** *Cert. Head*
Mrs Margaret Leverett *Cert. Asst.*
Miss Maud Cox *Uncert. Asst.*
Miss Florence Lake *Uncert. Asst.*
Miss Annie Cushing *Supplementary Asst.*
Miss Kathleen Simmonds *Student teacher*

May 6th 70 children absent without leave to attend Circus. They were reported to the Attendance Officer.

July 12th Children gave an entertainment in the Market Place as part of the War Savings Week Programme.

September 17th School closed at 2.45 p.m. to facilitate blackberry gathering by children.

October 21st **Mrs Leverett absent from school today because her husband is home on leave.**

November 1st **Many children absent through influenza. About 50 cases reported to the MOH & SMO.** [This was a serious national epidemic, killing thousands.]

Nov 4th **School medically closed.**

11th **92 present when school reopened.**

13th School closed again for three days.

18th School reopened again, 115 present.

19th School visited by Mr. Leafe. A number of members of staff absent through sickness.

20th School closed for Christmas.

1919

January 30th Miss Layern from the boys' department, helping out temporarily (until 4th Feb.) because of staff sickness. Miss Cushing ill, until 24th.

April 16th Diocesan Inspector's report: E. Vernon Smith remarks 'there seems to be an excess of fear, lest a mistake should be seen to be made'.

May 14th Children sent a wreath to Norwich for Nurse Cavell's funeral. They had previously contributed to the Cavell Memorial Fund, also bought a portrait of her, which now hangs in the school lobby.

11th July Miss Cox was absent part of the afternoon to go to the station with a party of London children, who had paid a visit to the neighbourhood for a fortnight past and made the acquaintance of our children.

21st July Seven children absent part of the afternoon, to attend eye clinic at boys' school.

October 8th Afternoon school opened at one o'clock and closed at ten minutes past three due to a circus being in town.

October 14th, 15th and 16th Doctor's routine visits.

October 31st School closed today for the holiday given to celebrate 'Peace'.

November 11th Appropriate lessons given throughout the day to commemorate the signing of the Armistice on November 11th 1918. School opened at one o'clock and closed at three-forty. Members of Urban District Council visited the school at three o'clock and distributed medals to children.

December 19th Children gave an entertainment to each other this afternoon. Afterwards made a collection for Dr. Elsie Inglis memorial for mother and child welfare.

1920

11th & 12th February **The morning and afternoon sessions were of two and a quarter hours length to allow of attendance at a bazaar. NEC gave permission.**

April 29th **HMI Mr Fear, Mr Key and Captain Parker visited the school. The object was instructing the teachers on the new physical exercises.**

May 31st **Major H. E. Holmes examined the registers.** [This is the first time Major Holmes appears in the logbooks. He continued to examine the registers for many years.]

1921

March 31st **Laura Cushing resigns the Headship of this school after 20 years happy service.**

Retirement of Head Teacher Laura Cushing (commenced as Head Teacher 1st January 1901; retired 1921). Kneeling: Annie Cushing (commenced as supplementary teacher 2nd February 1903, retired 1934). Back row: Dorothy Baker (pupil teacher), Maud Cox, Florrie Lake.

April 28th **Maud Atkins commenced Headship of girls' school.**

July 21st **School closed all day for Church Sunday school treat.**

September 12th

Staff:		
Miss Maud Atkins *Certified Head*	**Standard (class) VII**	
Miss Olive Jarvis *Certified Assistant*	VI	
Miss Maud Cox *Uncertified Assistant*	V	
Miss Alice Spencer *Uncertified Assistant*	I	

Miss Florence Lake *Uncertified Assistant*   III
Miss Annie Cushing *Supplementary*   II
Miss Mary Stanford *Student Teacher*   VIa
Miss Dorothy Baker *Pupil Teacher*

October 24th The girls of standard one and two went to the Vicarage Rooms for lessons all morning due to repairs being undertaken on their roof.

27th School Nurse excluded 20 children for 'verminous heads'.

3 & 4 November The school nurse once again visited the school and examined the children's heads, this time re-excluded 17 again.

23rd November and December 1st The school nurse revisited, but no exclusions reported.

16th Timetable suspended in order to prepare for the school party in the evening.

1922

January 11th School dentist visited for inspection only. [He returned on 25th, 26th, 27th and 30th; these visits were for treatment it may be assumed.]

January 12th School nurse visited.

28th February Holiday all day for Princess Mary's wedding.

6th March Dr Townend, District Medical Officer, visited school and inspected outside offices [lavatories].

13th Dr Nash, Chief Medical Officer, visited the school with Dr Townend and inspected the outside offices.

May 2nd Mr Read, Committee's Inspector, and Rev. Keeling Scott visit the school owing to complaints about the school's cleanliness.

May 18th Nit nurse inspected heads, Dr Kenway Williams visited and inspected outside offices.

19th Head, Miss Maude Atkins, absent from school during morning, owing to slight attack of malaria.

25th [Another visit from School Nurse and again on June 1st and on 23rd visited and inspected heads of all children present.]

June 14th, 15th and 20th **Dr Bryce** [the first woman doctor to visit as Assistant School Medical Officer].

20th June **The After-Care Committee met at the school.**

August 1st **Winifred Daborn started work as a pupil teacher at this school.** [Later to be Mrs Mueller.]

September 12th **Return of the school nurse for the day.**

Oct. 5th **The District Medical Officer visited, to examine children who seemed likely to have scarlet fever.**

6th **School closed for 14 days because of scarlet fever epidemic by Chief Medical Officer.**

Dec 14th **2 p.m. to 4 p.m. school open to parents for parents to visit to see the Christmas decorations and children at work.**

1923

Jan 29th to February 2nd **Rehearsals for the concert at the cinema. Needlework and handwork lessons were used for concert decorations and outfits etc.**

7th February **School times rearranged so as to fit in the afternoon concert at the cinema.**

5th **Mr Davis, Secretary to the Education Committee, inspected playground lavatories and school cleanliness.**

March 19th **School nurse examined 141 in total. Found 33 infestations of nits, but no other live vermin found.** [Nurse visited again on 16th April, but no other comment made in book.]

26th **School closed for whole day holiday, granted for wedding of the Duke of York (to Elizabeth Bowes-Lyon).**

20th June **Dentist visited.**

18th September **Ringworm clinic held in school (believed to be the first).**

25th October **The first year girls visited Swaffham Church in the charge of Miss Spencer as a continuation of their lessons on early buildings.**

November 30th & December 1st **Visit of school medical officer.**

1924

February 1st **Mr Fear visited the school and had a talk with the staff on short fortnightly tests, etc.**

May 2nd **Egg week and the girls sent 184 eggs to Swaffham Cottage Hospital.**

20th **Miss Maud Cox left after 20 years service. She took with her the hearty good wishes of the staff and girls on the occasion of her marriage.**

September 15th **School reopened after Harvest Holidays.**

16th **Nurse visited school and inspected every child present.**

30th **Mr Read visited school during afternoon session.**

October 21st **Nurse visited school and syringed the ears of five deaf children.**

November 13th **Dr Nash, Chief Medical Officer, and Dr Sexton, School Medical officer, visited the school, examined children's throats and order 'Closure' from 13th – 16th November (inclusive).**

17th **Closure ordered by telegram from Chief Medical Officer. Closure to last for one week.** [No reason given, but a teacher from Narborough was helping because her own school was closed because of Whooping Cough.]

December 10th **Half-holiday given and the whole school (with two exceptions) attended the performance of Peter Pan given by pupils of Swaffham Grammar School.**

1925

April 6, 7, & 8th **The children from the Infants School, who form the new Std. I in the Girls' School remain in the Infants' School for these three days, as the Std. I teacher, Miss A. Cushing, is absent through illness.**

May 27th **Mr Wilkinson, Physical Instruction Organiser, visited school during afternoon session – gave B. B.** [blackboard?] **Demonstration to staff – also practical demonstration of indoor physical exercises & country dances.**

September 7th **Miss Doris Houghton & Miss Elsie Lawrence commenced work as Student Teachers.**

November 11th **The whole school marched down to the War Memorial for the observation of the two minutes silence.**

1926

January 22nd **Information received that Mrs Weeks (Head Mistress) will not be able to return to school at all owing to serious operation. Her notice expires at end of February and until such time as a new Head Mistress is appointed, I am in charge.**

(Signed) Olive Yeardon (Cert. Assistant).

May 3rd **E. W. Campbell begins duty as Head Mistress today.** [A limited number of entries. Report of the HMI from last year was put in the book and is quite lengthy. 'The school has a pleasant atmosphere and very good tone and great care is taken to make the surroundings interesting and attractive.' Standards reached in the elementary work are decidedly below the normal, due to sickness amongst staff and pupils. A 'Super-Top' class had been created to help those of good ability, but this was not seen to be beneficial by the inspector, involving rapid promotion for many pupils whose work, even the most advanced class, was of inferior quality.]

Aug 5th **Only 83 girls present because of the Baptist Sunday school treat to Sheringham.**

September 13th **18 girls attended the advanced course in laundry.**

November 11th **The two minutes silence observed throughout the school.**

1927

February 3rd **The junior classes std. I to IV had an open afternoon. Several parents visited the school and watched the children at work.**

24th & 25th **Miss D. White, an assistant at the boys' school came to help with std. III & IV.** [Miss White started teaching in Swaffham in 1918 and was still teaching here until 1955, becoming probably the longest serving teacher in the history of our schools.]

March 31st The senior classes had an open afternoon.

May 26th The children attended Ascension Day, the school attended the children's service in the church from 9 to 9.30.

30th Three teams were entered for the country dance competition which was held on the Saturday in Norwich. Two of them gained 80% of the marks and so won certificates issued by the English Folk-Dancing Society.

July 20th School closed for the afternoon session, Castle Acre Pageant. [No more is mentioned about this, but a photograph exists.]

September 9th **Raffia requisition arrived.** [This is the first mention of this in the books.]

Miss E. D. Campbell C.H, Miss M.A. L. Bunn UA, Miss F. Lake UA, Miss D.Q. Baker UA, Miss A. Cushing Supplementary.

November 18th Two children sent home at 9.30 a.m. with impetigo on faces.

28th One child sent home at 9.30 with sores on her face.

1928

January 126 children on books.

26th 32 girls left school at 3 p.m. with permission of the Secretary, to attend a League of Nations concert at the cinema.

February 22nd **Ash Wednesday Church for service.**

March 8th **All the girls in standards 5, 6 & 7 to attend the cinema at 3 p.m. to see films shown by the RSPCA.**

April 2nd **County scholarship examination held at this school, 8 girls entered. 20 children sent up from the Infants' school.**

April 27th **Board of Education report.** [A very good report, praising the improved work done by the Headmistress and her teachers. A very good RI report.] **The following girls' handwriting slightly better, K. Layern, Maud Dye.** [K. Layern was Olive Wilson's mother.]

July 2nd School closed all day, on account of the 'Prince's Holiday' being kept. A wet morning and a day's outing organised for Co-operative Society employees led to a low attendance 117 from 144.

22nd October 18 girls sent on a two-day housewifery course.

24th October 18 girls sent on a three-day course in housewifery.

28th November Cookery classes now held in the laundry at the old workhouse. [The workhouse closed in 1929, but the buildings were used for such activities for a while.]

1929

January [Due to the snow, attendance varied from 89 to 100. There were 126 on the books.]

February [More snow, causing more absenteeism.]

April Number on books 138.

April [Diocesan exam results received and the best-written work included that of Dorothy Harrison in Standard 5 – she became Dorothy Butters, the author's mother.]

May 30th School was closed for general election.

November 8th Miss Anne Cushing is absent from school on account of the death of her sister, the late Head Teacher of this school.

1930

March 7th Many girls suffering from 'Pink eye', notification to school medical officer. [This epidemic lasted at least three, possibly four weeks, before it ceased being recorded in the log book. Attendance for the worst week was as low as 70.9%.]

April 1st 155 on books after admissions from the infants.

October 30th Two girls withdrawn by order of Dr Townend, question of diphtheria contact.

1931

January 5th Miss Margaret Jefferies began work as student teacher. [Later to be Mrs Steele, teaching until the 1950s.]

January 16th Medical inspection for girls with defect cards and log book cases.

31st March Ethel Campbell leaves her position as Head teacher. A temporary head was Miss E. F. Phillipson P.S.S.

June 15th HMI Miss Cooke's report received. 'The school has gone forward during the five years she [Miss Campbell] has been here, and there is evidence that hard and thorough work has been done. . . . She has won the loyalty and respect of both her staff and scholars, both of whom have cause to regret her departure.'

July 6th Miss Waterhouse (new headmistress) visited the school today.

8th Nurse inspected all 'card cases'.

September 7th School reopens, number on books 137.

Staff: Miss M. Waterhouse, L.L.A. (Hons) A.R. San. I. *Head*
         Miss M. A. Adam *CA*
         Miss Lake *UC*
         Miss Spencer *UC*
         Miss A Cushing *S*
         Miss M. Jefferies *ST*

Sept 17th I have today issued orders to Mr Jefferies, caretaker, in order to get satisfactory flushing in WCs.

December 1st The nurse visited and inspected every girl. Standard II was spoken to, owing to the number of dirty heads.

15th The senior girls are giving a short play in the Cinema this evening, so school closed at 3.30.

22nd Two large dressed dolls taken to the Cottage Hospital as Christmas gifts.

1932

January 11th **138 on roll.**

28th **The first time the girls visited the boys' Grammar School** [Hamond's], thanks to the courtesy of the headmaster, Mr Purdy. The occasion was a play the boys presented.

Violin classes from 5 – 6 pm commenced. The teacher was Miss Edmunds.

10th French circle commences today at 3 pm. The Tutor was M. M. Vallet.

April 5th As there was an interest in the Girl Guide movement, we are hoping to form a company in Swaffham. [22 girls had promised to join and prepare for guide work.]

May 6th Today the girls are hostesses to girls from Sporle, Dunham, and Pickenham at matinee 'Africa Speaks' at 4.15 p.m. in cinema. 500 scholars will be present.

May 10th 'Red Letter Day' school concert in cinema.

24th The first geographical expedition takes place after school today. The source of the River Nar at Tittishall visited and the stream and river traced as far as Narborough and the industrial aspect studied. Experiments and observations on speed of stream were made at various points. Headmistress in charge of girls.

26th A school branch of the Junior Red Cross Society was formed after school today.

29th A small party of senior girls went to Norwich Cathedral to a service celebrating the 21st birthday of the Guide movement.

July 5th School dentist in attendance for a few days. [Often these visits are for ten days.]

July 18th The county library van visited us and left 70 non-fiction books and 100 fiction books.

28th July At 3 p.m., at the end of term assembly, all the managers, ministers of the town, Mrs Heyhoe (lady magistrate) were present. The vicar presiding, many parents attended.

29th School closes for five weeks.

September 5th School reopens.

26th A party of 20 senior girls went with the headmistress to King's Lynn Theatre to see the 'Barretts of Wimpole Street'.

October 6th A party of senior girls is visiting Lynn this evening to see the film 'Palestine'.

I have organised a scholars' matinee at 4 p.m. in the cinema, when 'On Safari' a tale of central Africa will be shown, together with pictures of Scott's Centenary.

10th At 4 p.m. a party of senior girls visited Jermyn's needlecraft and rug-making exhibition.

A branch of Lloyd's bank was commenced today. Small amounts can be paid in to finance an educational trip next summer. 13/11d was paid in. Senior girls visited Lynn to see 'Midsummer Night's Dream'.

19th School Historical and geographical Society opens its winter session at 4 p.m. today. A series of slides have been arranged for from L.N.E.R. These lectures will take place monthly during the winter. The other weekly meetings will consist of debate and papers by the girls.

27th The School Debating Society started today with the subject 'The Seniors have Prep. from 6 to 7 p.m.'

Nov. 2nd A Pound Day Collection raised 120lb of goods. The House Captains, who were shown around the premises by matron, took all of this to the hospital.

8th A meeting of former pupils is called for this evening with the object of forming an 'Old Girls Association'.

9th The Senior Schoolgirls had a lantern slide show at 4 p.m. The slides coming from the L.N.E.R. The literary circle commences this evening.

17th The second winter session of the girls' French society opens at 4 p.m. today. The class in household science and hygiene for old girls of the school commences this evening.

22nd & 23rd School Medical Inspection.

28th The senior girls had a lantern talk on Norfolk in History and the slides were also shown to the Old Girls at 8 p.m.

Dec 5th A deputation from the Director of Agricultural Education came today. I promised to explore the possibilities of a course of evening lectures next Spring.

22nd The school gave 5 dramatic scenes this afternoon. The final scenes from 'The Merchant of Venice'.

23rd I gave the senior school a talk on the spirit of Christmas and Service for others. As a result, the seniors offered to undertake the Christmas collection for the Blind Institutions (House to House).

1933

8th February Miss Waterhouse tried the experiment of providing hot school meals for the girls from Cockley Cley. This was a great success, with 3 courses provided for 3d. per head. This was provided every Wednesday during the winter months.

15th Mid-week meals at a cost of 2d per head are to be provided for the rest of the term.

March 14th The school went to the cinema at 3.45 p.m. to be shown the film 'Back to Back'. The Junior Red Cross was inspected today by the County Commissioner (Mrs. Parker).

April 12th School collection of eggs for Swaffham Cottage Hospital.

May 3rd The Art Society spent the day at the crossroads at Weasenham Woods. The Historical Society visited Gt. Dunham church, an important Saxon church, and a week later they visited Newton church. On Saturday the House Captains were taken to see the Penn Pageant at Beaconsfield also Milton's cottage at Chalfont.

12th Mr Read visited the school with reference to school desks.

26th Fire drill was carried out this morning at 10.45. The school was clear in 2m. 10s.

July 14th House captains taken to see Bronte play in London.

Sept. 28th In connection with the Historical Society, the house captains were taken to see the prehistoric flint quarries (Grimes Graves) at Weeting at 4.30 p.m.

Nov. 15th After much preparatory work, a school branch of the 'League of Nations' was formed.

21st 90 girls saw a lantern talk on the 'Wild Life in Norfolk' in the Assembly Rooms.

Dec. 7th W. B. Rix spoke on 'Swaffham in the Past' at 4 p.m.

9th–11th 'Book Week' experiment, parents and friends were invited to school during the weekend. This was in order to get more suitable books read and bought for Christmas. A small selection of suitable books was on show, but not on sale. Also the senior Master at the Grammar School gave a talk on 'Juvenile Literature'.

1934

Jan. 11th A talk was given on the 'Last Ice Age' to the Senior Society. [Talks, lantern talks and visits to the cinema are very common now.]

14th The fourteen year-old girls were given a talk on 'personal' matters. This was followed by a visit to the hospital on April 18th and Matron talked to the girls on 'certain practical hygiene matters' in one of the private wards, as there is no opportunity to do so in school.

March 6th All the Junior school listened to 'A Year in the Life of a Bird' as an experiment with schools broadcasts.

25th Egg collection for Swaffham Hospital.

28th June The school took part in wild flowers competition in the local show. [First time children's section.]

July 12th League of Nations union members had a picnic at the 'Splashes'.

17th The results of the Temperance exam to hand today, show the school has won 11 prizes as against 6 last year.

Board of Education report : [The school was inspected on October 10th 1934 and other dates by Miss B. F. Cooke, HMI.] **'The school in general lacks facilities for Science, Arts & Crafts or for Practical Instruction in**

Housecraft, the room for this subject being a mile away from the school The numbers of girls means that they are overcrowded. In the middle school there is an age range of two years. Individual activities are practically impossible. The formation of a NCC branch of the library, the use made of school visits and school journeys adds an impetus to the study of local history and geography. The establishment of a summer camp during the summer term, during which interesting records have been made and published in the school magazine. Besides the League of Nations and the Red Cross the Citizens' Guild. In connection with the latter, outsiders on matters of social and civic interest have given talks to the leavers. Use of the wireless was made for speech training and music demonstrations. The cinema was used for educational films. The school has acquitted itself well in interschool sports. A keen interest is shown in organised games.'

1935

March 29th Miss A. Cushing retires today after 32 years service in this school. At the end of the morning session, the vicar, Major Holmes and Mr Gould were present and a mahogany clock with Westminster chimes was presented to Miss Cushing as a token of appreciation and goodwill.

21st June At the area sports this evening (14 schools), we were fortunate in winning the shield.

22nd Five of our girls took part in the county sports today. Mabel Bond was 5th in the high jump doing 2 inches more than the area girl last year. She was knocked out at 4' 4".

October 26th Royal Wedding Day. Each class had a 'joy day' arranged for them. The seniors visited the cider works at Attleborough.

1936

7th January Hilda A. Crowther commenced duty at the beginning of the afternoon session, in the absence, owing to illness, of Miss Waterhouse the Headmistress.

15th A weak place was reported in the flooring of Miss Hopkins' classroom and was reported to the correspondent. In one place there is a hole, which is a danger to those using the room.

20th January **Headteacher returns.**

22nd **We are leaving school today at 3.50 p.m. to be at the cinema by 4 p.m. for the film 'David Copperfield'. The village schools have been invited to join us, charge 2d. each.**

30th January **We have today 'earthed' the wireless aerial; therefore there is no risk to the building from lightning.**

31st **I [Miss Waterhouse] terminate my duties as Headmistress today, having been appointed to a grade 4 Senior Girls school. Miss Hopkins also resigns today, so this means that the only permanent members of the staff on Monday morning will be the two uncertificated mistresses.**

3rd February **Edna Dodman began duty at the school this morning.** [Headmistress?]

12th **Major Holmes visited school, inspected leaky pipe in cloakroom, ordered man to repair same.**

18th **A pupil left the school after serious allegations of theft from her grandmother. Items involved included a gold watch, leather writing case, etc.**

9th March **Wynyard Browne superintended 13 children who entered for the junior scholarship examination.** [Mr Browne was the author of *The Holly and the Ivy* (1950), a play believed to be based on people living in the town at the time.]

19th March **The school closed at 3.45 p.m., by permission of the managers, in order to be at the cinema by 4 p.m. to see the film 'Clive of India'. Charge 2d each.**

23rd March **Margaret Evans, temporarily in charge as Mrs E. Dodman has been transferred to Aylsham Boys School. Major Holmes visited and said Mrs Cook was temporarily transferred from the boys' school.**

26th March **Senior girls received an invitation from the Headmaster of the Grammar School to attend the dress rehearsal of their play 'She Stoops to Conquer'. The Mistresses and about 20 girls attended.**

Miss Blamire will take charge here on the 1st April. Miss Cook remaining until school affairs are settled.

30th March **Miss Patterson and the Monday cookery class gave an excellent** and enjoyable tea party for the teachers at the Domestic Science Centre.

1st April Miss A. Blamire is appointed Headteacher of Girls' and Infants Schools combined from this date.

8th June The swings in the playground have been removed, being unsafe, and are stored at Mr. Plowright's.

9th June Nurse Welsted visited and examined all the children (164).

15th June Dr. Moss called to ask if children could do some dancing for Hospital Day. This is impossible.

4th July Swaffham area sports day. Swaffham girls and boys won the shield.

16th July 21 cases of coughs, colds and whooping cough. Dr. Townsend, MOH, came in school and ordered that all the children who had not had whooping cough should be sent home. This left only 72 children in school. The school opened at 1.15 and closed at 3.45 p.m. as many of the girls were taking part in the work organised for Hospital Week.

7th August Miss S. Blamire commenced duties as Certified Assistant Mistress. She had been Head Mistress of Little Dunham school for many years, but this is now closed.

17th September Miss S. Blamire was officially appointed as a Certified Assistant, £285 per year.

6th October Mrs Curdie called about 'Milk in Schools' scheme.

11th November Armistice Day Service held in school 19.40 to 11 & the two minutes silence observed.

10th December King Edward abdicated.

11th The percentage this week is 35% owing to measles.

21st Parents Day Infants and Juniors gave playlets, and the Senior Girls interspersed with part songs & carols. 100 new Hymnbooks were presented to the school by Miss Cushing, Old Girls and Friends.

1937

11th January School reopened, but there was much sickness in the town still

– measles, influenza, coughs and colds. 101 present out of 166.

22nd 25 children who had not had measles were excluded from school.

19th February Attendance still low at 64%, colds coughs and 'flu being the chief causes.

5th April Re-opened after Easter, admitted 12 new scholars in the morning and one in the afternoon, making 175 on books

11th May Closed school for Coronation and Whit week.

24th June School closed at 3.45 p.m. for the Church Fete. The Senior girls danced the maypole dances.

30th June Lady dentist gave lecture to whole school on Care of Teeth – very much enjoyed and appreciated.

15th July School opened at 1.15 owing to Flower show. Several girls entered bunches of wild flowers & 5 prizes were taken.

16th Rev. J. C. Oakley took a scripture exam and told the senior girls that they knew more than any others he had examined & were quite the best he had seen.

28th School closes for the Sunday school outing to Hunstanton the next day.

6th September [6 girls had left because they were over 14, and two had left to go to East Dereham High School – first mention of Dereham High.]

3rd November Children asked to contribute to Hospital 'Pound Day' – a splendid response and 25 senior girls took load to the Hospital at 2 p.m.

16th December A parents' & visitors' afternoon held. Many parents availed themselves of the opportunity of seeing their children's productions. The room was full to overcrowding. The Vicar was Chairman & Major Holmes & Mr. Shingles both spoke. Lady Roberts of Cockley Cley Hall & Mr Purdie, from the Grammar School, were also there.

23rd Today, I (A. Blamire) & my sister (Miss S. Blamire) resign our posts in this school. The managers (Chairman, the Vicar) & parents assembled in the afternoon & a presentation was made. We thank, from our hearts, all who have been so kind to us, & especially the Managers who have done everything to help to help the work to proceed happily.

School closed for Christmas.

1938

10th January Edna Dodman commenced temporary duty in this school this morning.

5th April Piano belonging to Mr Copeman was removed from school to the Vicarage.

1st June Dorothy G. Wright commenced duty [as head teacher] this morning.

20 September [Dr Platt's Board of Education report:] 'There are 152 children from 4 to 14 years of age in attendance. The boys are transferred to the Swaffham Boys' Church of England Department at about the age of 7. There are five classes, 2 of infants, 2 of juniors and 1 of senior pupils. The Infants are accommodated in a separate building at one end of the playground. Of the three rooms at their disposal, two are in constant use as classrooms. In regard to musical activities the teachers are considerably handicapped through lack of a piano or gramophone. The remaining classes are housed in a building, which contains a large partitioned main room and two classrooms. Half the main room is available for activities, but unfortunately a good deal of valuable space is taken up by surplus furniture, and other school equipment, for which no other storage accommodation is provided. It would be well, however, further to develop the training on lines in accordance with modern junior school practice, the subjects of art and crafts, oral English and music offer opportunities in this direction. The senior class comprises 38 children from 11 to 14 years of age. The oldest girls are organised as a separate group within the class and do a good deal of private study, working on assignments prepared the teacher. The girls are taught Housecraft at a nearby centre, which they attend on one half day a week. The Head Teacher is aware of the desirability of strengthening the instruction in Art & Craft, including needlecraft, & is taking steps to bring about an improvement in this important branch of the training.'

1939

9.1.39 Opened school.

1.2. Closed school this afternoon owing to influenza epidemic.

13.2 Re-opened school. [Very brief notes – March 31st to September 11th covered in one page.]

Oct 5 The dentist examined all the children present 116, also the 21 evacuees.

[First mention of evacuees – no reference to war.]

Nov 8th **Dentist extracting teeth today.**

Nov. 28th **Surplus furniture removed to E. Dereham & N. Pickenham schools. Also several sets of text books for evacuees.**

1940

May 10th **Closed at noon for Whitsun Holiday.**

14th **Resumed school – holiday cancelled owing to war.**

Aug 2nd **Closed at 3.45 for summer holidays.**

Sept 9th **Re-opened school.**

Oct 17th **Closed at noon owing to school being used for inspection of evacuees.**

18th **Closed for cleaning.**

21st **Closed for evacuees.**

Nov 1st **Closed for evacuees.**

Nov. 25th **Received from Ashill School 14 tables & 28 chairs L.C.C. property.**

Dec. 18th **Received from Raynham School 4 dual desks & 2 long tables. Received from Ashill School desks lent from this school.**

1941

Feb 17th **Infants 7 years & under excluded for measles.**

27 **Closed half day for evacuees.**

28 **Closed for cleaning school.**

Mar 7th **Raid warning at 11 a.m. – lasting until 4.10 pm. Registers closed at 3 p.m. – very few children at school.**

12th **Raid warning on at 9 a.m. Registers marked at 9.30 a.m.**

March 25 **169 children immunised against diphtheria, 240 on roll.**

May 22nd Closed for half day for reception of evacuees.

23rd Closed for school cleaning.

26th Re-opened school. Cleaning after reception of evacuees was not satisfactory – floors should have been scrubbed. Infants' school floors were covered with food grease & floors in four rooms had been urinated upon, to a disgusting state, & should have been well cleansed for the protection of our children.

30th Closed at noon (12.30) for Whit holiday.

June 9th Re-opened school & found it still unscrubbed.

20th School has now been scrubbed in worst dirty parts.

July 3rd Commenced school at 1.30 p.m. and closed at 3.45 (Secretary's orders) so that youth service meeting could be held there.

10th A 3 yr. old evacuee slipped and injured his chin, Dr. Hall-Smith called & put three stitches into the wound.

July 7th Mrs Blowers commenced work today, one hour daily, washing up milk mugs & utensils.

21st Miss Prouton attending Special course for Infant teachers at Dereham.

22nd [After a critical report on Religious Instruction by Rev. Mr Hughes, the Head Teacher added a note:] **Owing to the large classes in the school, due to wartime evacuation, the children were talked to generally on religion & not questioned in detail upon the syllabus of work covered during the year. Thus the examiner's remarks seem to convey a wrong impression. Infants' schemes could have been produced, if asked for, & each class had covered its Old Testament scheme from the Cambridge Syllabus.**

1942

Kindertransport

An exercise book exists, with 'ENGLISH MEASLES VACCINATION RECORD" on the cover and 'Cockley Cley (Old School)' in pencil, but crossed through and 'Swaffham Junior and Infants 1954' written above. Inside, on the first page and a half are the names of 25 children, most of whom were brought back from Hackney by the (then) Dowager Lady Roberts, grandmother of Sir Samuel Roberts, to Cockley Cley Hall. The children were mainly European Jewish children, who had been lucky enough to be sent on sealed trains by their families to England. All were under 17 years of age. Over that age, the Nazis would not let them go.

There were also children in Cockley Cley who had been evacuated in 1939. Two brothers and a sister, at least, came with two teachers. They all went to Cockley Cley School. One of the brothers in a letter in Swaffham Museum wrote of Lady Roberts knitting him socks and a scarf and buying him savings stamps. They were all well looked after and enjoyed their time in Cockley Cley.

Jan 21st **The girls attended films by the Ministry of Information.**

Feb 20th **School closed owing to lack of fuel.**

30th April **Miss Wright absent. (Injured in air raid.)**

14th May **Ascension Day and the children attended a short service in the church during the RI period 9 – 9.40 a.m.**

July 1st **Head Teacher returned to duty after approx. 3 months spent recovering from injuries sustained during an air raid. School opened at 1 p.m. and closed at 3.15 in order those children could take part in the Garden Fete for Church School Funds.**

July 13th **School received piano.**

28th **Nurse visited for scarlet fever survey.**

25th November **Nurse examined all children present for dirty heads & sore throats (from 9.30 to 3.30).**

26th **Mrs Easter, a civil defence worker, lectured on poison gases (10.15 a.m. to 11.15).**

December 1st **Drs. Hall-Smith, Thorpe & Moss(e), inoculated 40 children against diphtheria.**

9th **Again cleaner has not done her work properly. Infant school fires only just alight at 9.30 a.m., & one completely out. Room not used today as cleaner refused to come and light fire. This is not the first occasion on which the classes have been disorganised thus.**

1943

February 18th School closed, no coal.

March 30 **Miss Wright returned Monday afternoon – wartime transport difficulty delayed return on Sunday.**

May 11th **Cookery class returned to school owing to a mistake of date made by the Castle Acre class.**

25th **Cleaner refused to sweep school but it was cleaned by her paid helper.**

26th **School not swept. Teachers each cleaned own room the next morning.**

27th **Teachers again swept own rooms, but cleaner came in evening & did them again.**

[Dissension between Head Teacher & cleaner, owing to cleaner refusing Head Teacher access to coal-house, & taking the keys off the school premises during school hours. Coalman kept waiting for ¼ hr while cleaner brought the keys. Workman had to go back to town for a pail. Teachers had no implements to mop up flooded cloakroom, nor brooms to brush up children's vomit. Hence Head Teacher insisting that keys should be hung up on premises during school hours. Cleaner asserts that managers told her to take away keys. Duplicate keys now purchased by the Head Teacher.]

May 31st **It seems that the L.C.C. Administrative Officer came after school hours & removed L.C.C. furniture.**

June 11th **Cleaner has done no morning dusting, nor been to unlock school since May 25th.**

28th Twenty girls exempted from school in order to pick peas at Carol House Farm.

July 1 **Girls returned to school.**

6th Pea picking again today.

8th School closed at 3.17 p.m., so that girls could go to Church School Fete.

9th **Children warned again about touching strange objects, which might be explosives.**

26th Twenty girls went to Hill Farm, Dunham for fruit picking for one day.

September 6th Re-opened school. Infants school has not been scrubbed therefore three infant classes and teachers are working in one room in the girls' school & work is much disorganised.

9th Commenced afternoon school at 1 o'clock so that girls could help at the local hospital fete.

Nov. 3rd Re-opened school (after half-term holiday) no fires alight, cleaner has apparently resigned again. [During the war years there was several changes in teaching staff. Only the changes of the Head Teacher have been noted here.]

Dec 14th Fire-lighting most unsatisfactory, paper & wood not burnt through at 10.30 a.m., and temperatures of rooms all below 40°, this has been happening all the term (and on one day only have the thermometers shown 60°) this means that children are too cold to benefit from their lessons.

1944

January 10th Re-opened school, cleaning not completed, owing to ceiling repair not being done. Infant cloakroom flooded and unusable today. Washing for Dec. 20 – 23rd not done. Cleaner resigned.

11th Work disorganised, as no fires & no cleaning done & school left open all night.

12th Temporary cleaner commenced work.

27th School closed – no coal.

28th School closed – no coal.

31 Opened school, 10 cwt of coal delivered.

Feb 2nd Cookery class cancelled – no coal.

May 22nd Dr. O'Connor holding medical inspection each afternoon until June 5th.

July 13th Talk to leavers (boys included) by officials from the Labour Bureau.

14th School closed in afternoon for reception of evacuees from London.

19th Girl leavers interviewed by a Miss Vicars from the Labour Exchange.

Oct 12th **Meeting of managers, county architect and Heads of Schools about new canteen site on school garden.**

Oct 26th **An LCC teacher reported here at 9 a.m., but only to announce that she was returning to London, as she was not satisfied with her billet.**

Dec 14th **Two LCC assistants were to start but both postponed and then cancelled.**

1945

Jan 25th **LCC assistant arrived yesterday and starts work today. (Returned to London on 28th March.)**

May 8th & 9th **School closed for Victory in Europe.**

[*May 10th* It seems Miss Wright has left her position as Head Teacher, as a different writing style is now used. There is no mention of the name of the successor.]

18th **King's Lynn Special Grammar School exams held in Girls School.**

22nd July **Daphne Mallett and Joan Nason heard that they had been successful in the Secondary Schools Examination (Dereham High School).**

26th **School closed in afternoon, but all girls and Infants attended to give a Physical Training Display for the Welcome Home Fund. Parents and friends were invited.**

25th and 26th October **School closing for VJ holidays.**

HERE ENDS OUR TRANSCRIPTION – FOR NOW.
THE SCHOOL CONTINUED IN EXISTENCE UNTIL 1977, WHEN
SWAFFHAM HAMONDS COMPREHENSIVE SCHOOL WAS FORMED FROM THE FORMER
SWAFFHAM SECONDARY MODERN SCHOOL AND HAMOND'S GRAMMAR SCHOOL.
HIGHLIGHTS FROM THE NATIONAL SCHOOL LOG BOOKS
HAVE ALSO BEEN TRANSCRIBED DOWN TO 1977
SO AS TO BE AVAILABLE FOR WIDER PUBLICATION IN DUE COURSE.

Index

Note: Names of teachers (even if only temporary or pupil teachers) are shown in *italics*. An asterisk * against an entry indicates that the subject is mentioned too frequently and briefly for all occurrences to be indexed; the page numbers given are for the earliest, representative and most detailed mentions.

Lightning Source UK Ltd.
Milton Keynes UK
UKOW06f1107081215

264331UK00002B/103/P